CHRIST
IN MODERN ATHENS

CHRIST
IN MODERN ATHENS

THE CONFRONTATION OF CHRISTIANITY WITH MODERN CULTURE AND THE NON-CHRISTIAN RELIGIONS

BY

DR C. J. BLEEKER

Professor of the History and Phenomenology of Religions
at the University of Amsterdam

LEIDEN
E. J. BRILL
1965

To

J. J. VAN DEN BROEK
who encouraged me
to write this book

CONTENTS

                                                        Page

Preface   IX

Paul on the Areopagus   1
    Paul's Significance.   2
    Paul's Journey to Athens   5
    The Sermon on the Areopagus   5
    The Value of the Sermon   8
    Theological Justification   10
    Intentional Exegesis   17
    Three Motifs   23

Christ in Modern Athens.   26

The Christian Attitude towards Modern Culture   37
    Towards a Definition of Culture   41
    Triumphs of the Intellect   47
    The Christian Attitude towards Modern
    Culture   54

The Christian Evaluation of the Non-Christian
Religions   60
    A Historical Insights   61
    B Assessment of Viewpoints   81
        (1) All Religions Are False   84
        (2) All Religions Are Equally True . . .   86

(3) Only Christianity Is True   90
   (a) Karl Barth's Standpoint   91
   (b) Henrik Kraemer's Attitude   . . .   98
   (c) Conclusion   106
C The Evaluation of the Non-Christian Religions   107

The Future of Religion   127
   Religion   127
   Christianity   140
   Christianity and the Non-Christian Religions 147

PREFACE

A journey abroad, embarked upon in the spirit of adventure, has a curious effect on the traveller. On the one hand he broadens his horizons and thus casts off some of the prejudices and habits, characteristic of the environment in which he was born and raised, while on the other the contrast between his own way of life and that of his foreign friends makes the characteristic traits in his nature stand out in relief and he discovers himself to be a typical citizen of his native land. These experiences are not as contradictory as they might seem. In actual fact all that happens is that the traveller becomes more keenly aware of the true nature of his reactions and convictions in strange surroundings.

The study of the history of religions and of the phenomenology of religion has a similar effect. The belief, even the fear, is widespread that a Christian who immerses himself in non-Christian forms of religion and learns to appreciate and even admire their beauty and profundity runs the risk of losing his faith. In reality the opposite is true. Anyone who seriously devotes himself to the study of alien religions will soon find that he can never fully comprehend them because he can never identify himself spiritually

with, say an ancient Egyptian, a Manichee, a Buddhist
or a Muslim. What the encounter with the non-
Christian religions does enable him to do, however,
is to discover the true structure and unique significance of his own Christian faith.

It may sound paradoxical but it is nevertheless a
fact that the proper study of the history of religions
and of the phenomenology of religion leads or even
forces the Christian to discover himself as a believer,
while in the second instance it causes him to ponder
the significance of Christianity today.

These subjects open our eyes to three connected
truths: First, that religion is essential to human life.
However widespread disbelief may be, and however
many well-founded objections may be raised to the
quality of mankind's religious concern in the past
and present, the whole history of religions proves that
human life loses its meaning if the belief in a higher
reality dies. Secondly, that it has been man's constant
endeavour to find the true faith, the ultimate religion.
Since religion is a human phenomenon, a product of
culture, it is obvious that every form of religion is
subject to human short-sightedness and sinfulness.
Yet true believers have always sought a living religion. Hence the student of the history of religions
must always search for the inner core of the exotic religious phenomena that he is studying. Thirdly, that
religion has only been able to maintain itself through

the centuries because it has constantly renewed itself, and so it follows that the existing religions must undergo a process of self-purification if they wish to find a hearing in this day and age for the truth that they proclaim.

The logical consequence of these insights is that we begin to ask ourselves in our present religious situation: first, how does the Christian faith to which we profess compare with other forms of religion which are evidently in like measure the staff of life to their respective adherents? And secondly, what should Christianity's attitude be towards modern culture? These two questions are closely allied for the simple reason that the confrontation between Christianity and the non-Christian religions takes place in the mental climate of our time. That this climate will have its effect both on Christianity as such and on the Christian evaluation of the non-Christian religions is self-evident.

Such may be said to be the theme of this book. The subject is Christianity today and the attitude appropriate to the Christian faith in the twentieth century or, to be more precise, the confrontation between Christianity and modern culture and Christianity and the non-Christian religions. The title conveys this idea more succinctly: Christ in modern Athens. The considerations mentioned above will provide some explanation why an historian of religion has felt called upon to express his views on questions which are usually deemed to be beyond his scope. The fact is that this subject has been of absorbing interest to me for many years now. The historian of religion is, after all, not only an impartial observer, who casts a cold scientific eye on his material, but he also feels deeply involved in the religious truths and values with which he has become acquainted in the course of his studies. This implies that his investigations can lead him to ask questions, the answers to which lie beyond the bounds of his profession. If, however, he clearly indicates where the border line between his own field and other fields of scholarship lies, he is undoubtedly entitled to seek an answer to the questions that have arisen in his mind. As a Christian he will strive to find a Biblical justification for this answer, not merely to play it safe scripturally, but because he is convinced that no decision can be correct and beneficial unless it is an expression of evangelical truth.

Now, over a period of time I have grown to believe that Paul's famous sermon on the Areopagus contains a number of principles upon which a new approach to the aforementioned problems could be based. Acts 17 tells of Paul's activities in the Athens of his time. We are concerned with the implications of the presence of Christ in the Athens of our day.[1]

[1] In an attempt to develop a close argument I have restricted myself to matters of primary importance. References will occasionally be made in the notes to religio-historical and theological problems on which the argumentation touches.

PAUL ON THE AREOPAGUS

There are historians who maintain that it is impossible to write a history of ancient times. They point out that many facts concerning this distant past have been lost or intentionally suppressed. In their opinion the evidence is too scanty for us to be able to compose a reliable picture of those far-off days. Undoubtedly they are right when they say that our documentation from antiquity reveals an appalling number of lacunae. Yet the conclusion that they draw is open to question. Numerous substantial books and brilliant monographs prove that a vivid picture of antiquity may be evoked from scanty and unruly material.

In one respect, however, their thesis is irrefutable. It is rarely possible to describe the personalities and careers of the great figures of antiquity in a satisfactory way. What do we really know of the characters and lives of mighty rulers like Hammurabi, Sesostris III and Cyrus II, of a founder of a religion like Zarathustra, or of a philosopher like Plato? Little or nothing! Paul is an exception to this rule. Of all the figures from the early days of Christianity he is the most colourful. We know details of his career: his origins in Tarsus, his schooling as a scribe, his conversion on his way to Damascus, his years of work in service of the gospel—three great missions, his imprisonment in Jerusalem, his voyage to Rome, where he wished to stand trial before the emperor, and his dealings with fellow Christians in the capital of the Roman Empire. Only an account of his end is lacking. His letters have made us familiar with the nature of his faith in Jesus Christ and with the structure of his theological ideas. Furthermore, the man Paul stands before us as a living human being with all his faults and all his virtues. The shortcomings in his character do not, however, prevent us from considering him as one of the greatest and most original personalities in the history of Christianity. Second Corinthians 12.2 where Paul speaks of being caught up into the third heaven gives us reason to suspect that the apostle had a tendency towards ecstasizing. To what extent he was a mystic, as Schweitzer maintains,[1] remains disputable. There is probably no one who will disagree with the proposition that he was a religious visionary, that is to say that it was his imaginative powers that enabled him to grasp the true meaning of the message of Jesus Christ.

PAUL'S SIGNIFICANCE

Paul was the first person fully to understand that the gospel was meant for the whole world and for the

[1] A. Schweitzer, *Die Mystik des Apostels Paulus*, 1930.

whole of humanity. From this he drew a conclusion which would have far-reaching consequences for Christianity: he began to devote himself entirely to preaching the gospel among the Gentiles. Perhaps he had a few unknown predecessors, but nevertheless he remains the great pioneer in this field, both on account of the passion with which he dedicated himself to this task and because of the fundamental theological justification which he gave to his mission. His origins in Tarsus, situated as it was within the realm of Hellenistic culture, and his Jewish upbringing made him eminently suitable for the missionary work he undertook, since they had bestowed upon him the necessary ability to adapt the gospel, which was rooted in the Jewish climate of thought, to the Greek way of thinking. Paul, who could at times be a difficult person, also combined with these qualities the flexibility of spirit that characterizes the true pastor. As he said himself he was able to speak to the Jews like a Jew, and behave like a Gentile among the Gentiles, who are outside the law (1 Cor. 9.19 ff.). He possessed this evangelical adaptabilty, without distorting his message or being untrue to himself, because he had understood more fully than anyone else that love is the crux of the teachings of Jesus Christ. Hence his advice to his followers not to offend those whose faith is weak with demonstrations of spiritual freedom (1 Cor. 8.1 ff.; 10.23 ff.) and his song of praise to love in 1 Cor. 13.

Theologically Paul was an original thinker. He interpreted the meaning of the person and teachings of Jesus Christ in a way that has continued to exercise a powerful influence on Christian theology right up until the present day. On his conversion Paul had learned to know Christ as the Lord to whose service he dedicated his life. This conversion was so complete that he entered into a spiritual communion with Christ. Thus he was redeemed from the power of evil, because he experienced in his own person the crucifixion and resurrection of our Lord. Hence he understood that man's sins can never be vindicated merely by his obeying the commandments of the law, but only by faith and by virtue of God's mercy, that is to say by entering into a pure relationship to God. Paul's faith bestowed upon him a share in the joy given by the Holy Spirit, and so he could confidently await the coming of the Kingdom of God.

This short sketch of Paul's highly original contribution to the propagation and interpretation of the gospel has been given for two reasons. First, to remind the reader of facts which he will already be acquainted with, and secondly, because this picture of Paul's mission to the heathens forms an indispensable backdrop to the sermon which Acts 17 tells us that he preached on the Areopagus.

PAUL'S JOURNEY TO ATHENS

There was nothing fortuitous about Paul's journey to Greece and his stay in Athens. It was the logical consequence of the view he took of his mission. Paul had apparently charged himself with the task of propagating the gospel throughout the Roman Empire. We read in his letter to the Romans, for example, that he planned to travel to Spain by way of Rome (Rom. 15.18). After visiting Asia Minor he doubtless felt the urge to cross to Macedonia and continue his journey to the celebrated Greek capital. Acts 16.8—10 records how one night at Troas on the Hellespont Paul received a vision of a Macedonian who cried out to him: 'Come across to Macedonia and help us.' This vision is sufficient proof of the fact that Paul considered his journey to Greece as a divine task. We need have no doubt that he fully understood the significance of his going to Athens. Although the city, even in his day, had already lost much of its former glory, it was still the focal point of Greek cultural life and the obvious setting for a confrontation between the gospel and the autonomous culture of the time. Paul's sermon on the Areopagus was to usher in this great event.

THE SERMON ON THE AREOPAGUS

As will be recalled, Acts 17 records how Paul, while

awaiting the arrival of Silas and Timothy, took a look
round Athens and was struck by the number of idols.
He entered into conversation with the Jews in the
synagogue and with "gentile worshippers", that is
with the proselytes, and with anyone he found on his
daily visits to the market-place. Among these persons
were a number of Epicurean and Stoic philosophers
who took Paul to the Areopagus to give him an opportunity to explain the new doctrine which sounded
so strange to them. Thus it came about that Paul delivered his well-known sermon.

This sermon has understandably become the subject of many, sometimes contradictory, exegetical dis-
cussions.[1] Scholars are agreed that the brief address
offered in Acts 17 may scarcely be called a sermon, and
that it is therefore dubious whether it is an accurate
account of what Paul said to a group of Athenians who
were curious to hear what this 'charlatan', as they

---

[1] E. Norden, *Agnostos Theos*, 1913; J. Weiss, *Die Schriften
des neuen Testaments*, 1917 III; A. Deissmann, *Licht vom Osten*,
1923; *Paulus*, 1925; M. Dibelius 'Paulus auf dem Areopag',
Sitzungsberichte der Heidelberger Akademie der Wissenschaften,
phil.-hist. Klasse, 1938—39. 2 Abh; M. Lackmann, *Vom Ge-
heimnis der Schöpfung*, 1952; B. Gärtner, *The Areopagus Speech
and Natural Revelation* 1955; H. L. Strack and P. Billerbeck,
Kommentar zum Neuen Testament aus Talmud und Midrasch II,
2nd ed. 1956; C. S. C. Williams, *A Commentary on the Acts of
the Apostles* (Harper's New Testament Commentaries) 1957;
H. P. Owen 'The Scope of Natural Revelation in Romans I
and Acts XVII', *New Testament Studies*, Vol. V, 1958-59.

called him, had to say for himself, and even whether this event took place on the Areopagus. That Paul preached in Athens is incontestable. It is only a question of what this sermon, as it now stands, is worth. Opinions differ widely on two points: First, is this a preaching of the gospel adapted to the Greek way of thinking or does this address contain a Greek doctrine of natural revelation, which has been given a Christian veneer? Secondly, is it really conceivable that Paul spoke in the spirit of this sermon? As representatives of the two opposing schools of thought A. Deissmann and M. Dibelius may be quoted. Deissmann writes:

> Ich fand, dass das grösste Missionsdokument des Neuen Testaments, die Paulusrede auf dem Areopag in Athen, darauf berechnet (war) dem grossstädtischen Heidentum der Mittelmeerwelt das Charakteristische der neuen Religion in knappster Form vorzuführen... Dass die Rede kein Stenogramm ist, ist ebenso wahrscheinlich, wie sie sicher paulinischen Geist offenbart und ein geradezu welthistorisches Manifest in der Geschichte der Religionen und der Religion ist... Jede Predigt der Missionare war, wie die Areopagrede, Christuspredigt, und jeder Hörer der Missionare empfand: sie bringen den Christuskult.[1]

After a careful analysis of the contents and style of the sermon Dibelius comes to the conclusion:

---

[1] Deissmann, *op. cit.*, pp. 329, 331.

> Die Areopagrede ist eine hellenistische Rede mit christlichem Schluss: ihr Thema ist die Gotteskenntnis, zu der jeder Mensch gelangen kann. ...von dem Anspruch der christlichen Botschaft, die wahre Gotteserkenntnis erst durch Offenbarung zu besitzen und mitteilen zu können, wird nichts gesagt... So erweist sich die Areopagrede in ihrem—auf das Ganze gesehen—rationalen Charakter als ein Fremdling im Neuen Testament.[1]

Dibelius neither wishes nor is able to deny the presence of evangelical overtones in the sermon: Paul exhorts his audience to repentance with a view to the approaching judgement which will be passed in God's name by 'a man of his choosing; of this he has given assurance to all by raising him from the dead', words that obviously refer to Jesus without explicitly mentioning his name. Therefore, to my mind, it is by no means unthinkable that Paul should have spoken in this vein in Athens and taken as his starting-point the uncommon reverence for the gods displayed by the Athenians—as witnessed *inter alia* by the altar-inscription 'To an Unknown God'—in order to reveal to his audience the true nature of the God whom they worshipped without knowing Him.

THE VALUE OF THE SERMON

Be this as it may, the value of this sermon is not

[1] Dibelius, *op. cit.*, p. 36.

determined by our attitude to these points of con-
troversy. Nor by the undeniable fact that Paul met
with little or no success in Athens, apart from the
conversion of Dionysius, the Areopagite, a woman
named Damaris and a number of other men. In all
events a church did not arise. Despite this Deissmann
has justly called the sermon 'Das grösste Missions-
dokument des Neuen Testaments', 'ein geradezu
welthistorisches Manifest in der Geschichte der Re-
ligionen und der Religion'. And Dibelius, who feels
obliged to acknowledge that 'die folgenden christlichen Generationen haben den wirklichen Paulus
missverstanden—diesen von Lukas geschaffenen Are-
opagredner haben sie verstanden', gives evidence of
having an eye for the significance of Paul's appearance
on the Areopagus when he concludes:

> Paulus auf dem Areopag—das bedeutet nicht eine
> historische, sondern eine symbolische Begegnung.
> Die Areopagrede ward zum Wahrzeichen christlicher
> Theologie auf dem Boden griechischer Geistesbil-
> dung.[1]

Although it is not unreasonable to argue about the
historical character of the story of Paul's visit to
Athens, for our present purposes this is of minor importance. What concerns us is that this was the first
confrontation between the gospel and the autono-

[1] *Ibid.*, p. 56.

mous culture of that day. Paul or if one prefers, the writer of Acts 17 was conscious of this. The sermon is apparently attuned to this fact, and as a consequence Paul's words contain elements which may be brought to bear upon the great issues that occupy us today, namely the attitude Christianity should adopt towards the culture of our own time on the one hand and towards the non-Christian religions on the other.

THEOLOGICAL JUSTIFICATION

A Christian who is serious about his faith feels obliged to let his attitude be governed by the truths of the gospel, that is to say he wishes to live and act in a theologically justifiable fashion. For his relationship to God and to his fellow men, for his behaviour within his community, the New Testament gives many and explicit precepts. The difficulties and uncertainties arise when he is confronted with the problem of how he can justify his attitude towards modern culture and the non-Christian religions according to evangelical principles.

What, we ask ourselves, are the precepts offered by the Gospels for the solution of these problems? With regard to the question of what a Christian's attitude to modern culture should be, our findings will largely depend on the view we have of the purport of the Gospels, in other words on the weight we place on

the eschatological tenor of Jesus' teachings. Even if
one does not subscribe to Schweitzer's thesis of 'kon-
sequente Eschatologie',[1] it cannot be denied that
Jesus' life was dominated by the expectation of the
coming of the Kingdom of God. Accordingly, it is
understandable that he did not devote much attention
to the affairs of this world. The principles of justice,
truth, brotherly love and peace, which are the standards of our society, may in themselves be derived
from the conception of the Kingdom of God. But
then the evangelical expectation concerning the Kingdom of God must first be stripped of its eschatological
connotations.[2] Added to this is the fact that Jesus
belonged to a relatively simple society so that the
complicated questions which arise within our modern
culture were naturally unknown to him. Hence we
cannot expect to find in his message clear precepts for
Christian behaviour in the complex world of our day.

If we search the Gospels for lines to guide us in our
attitude to the non-Christian religions, we make the
following discovery: from various passages it emerges
that Jesus largely restricted his work to his own people.

[1] A. Schweitzer, *Die Geschichte der Leben-Jesu-Forschung*, p.
390f.

[2] It would seem unnecessary, and within the framework of
this book unfeasible, to go into the problems arising from the
eschatological expectations of the New Testament, let alone
to discuss critically the various standpoints adopted in that
connection. Furthermore, this question will be raised once again
in another context.

When he sent out the disciples he instructed them as follows: 'Do not take the road to gentile lands, and do not enter any Samaritan town; but go rather to the lost sheep of the house of Israel' (Matt. 10.5, 6). He refused at first to drive an unclean spirit out of the daughter of a Syrophoenician woman, saying that 'it is not fair to take the children's bread and throw it to the dogs.' It was only through quick-wittedness and faith that the woman persuaded him to grant her request (Mark 7.24—30). In the parallel story in Matthew he clearly indicated the limits of his task with the words: 'I was sent to the lost sheep of the house of Israel, and to them alone' (Matt. 15.21—28). On the other hand, he was quick to acknowledge the genuine faith of the centurion from Capernaum (Matt. 8.5—13; Luke 7.1—10). When he was refused entrance to a Samaritan village and the disciples wished to punish the villagers with fire from heaven, Jesus rebuked them (Luke 9.15—56). In the overfamiliar parable of the good Samaritan a Gentile set the example for true mercifulness (Luke 10.25—37). Furthermore Jesus anticipated that with the coming of God's Kingdom many would come from east and west to feast with Abraham, Isaac, and Jacob in the Kingdom of Heaven (Matt. 8.11; Luke 13.28—29).

Such passages show that Jesus did not think along purely nationalistic lines, but was willing to credit Gentiles likewise with true faith, although he knew that he had been especially called to proclaim the gospel among his own people. Jesus' well-known command to his disciples to go forth and preach the gospel (Matt. 28.6 f.; Luke 24.46 f.; Mark 16.15) is, even if the words are authentic, too general in its purport for it to be able to serve as a guide to the solution of the complicated problem of the relationship between Christianity and the non-Christian religions as this confronts us today. The same applies to the words from the Gospel according to John which are frequently quoted in answer to this question. Jesus' statement: 'I am the way; I am the truth and I am life; no one comes to the Father except by me' (14.6) is apparently addressed directly to his audience and is an exhortation to the *imitatio Christi*. For Christians Christ is indeed the true way to God. These words of Jesus are the call of a preacher and not a mere article of faith. We would be depriving them of their essential qualities if we were to draw from them the conclusion that, apart from the way pointed out by Jesus, no other means of acquiring knowledge of God exists. Did not Jesus also say: 'No man can come to me unless he is drawn by the Father who sent me' (6.44), a statement that presupposes that God addresses himself directly to man and thus belies the notion that knowledge of God through revelation is exclusive.[1] Our conclusion must therefore be that, as was the case with

[1] In point of fact the discussion of this Johannine quotation

the Christian appraisal of modern culture, the Gospels do not give any practical indications of how our attitude towards the non-Christian religions should be determined.

Similarly, Paul's letters do not offer us anything directly applicable to the solution of these problems either. In his own attitude to worldly affairs Paul shows his respect for the authorities and the *status quo* in Rom. 13.1—7. This passage which has repeatedly been subjected to exegesis and almost equally often misused does not offer much support, when we consider that Paul, as is evident from his letters, looked upon the world as transitory, because he was awaiting the end of this aeon, the second coming of the Lord and the resurrection of the dead (1 Cor. 15.1 f.). Hence we cannot assume in Paul's letters a positive and critical interest in the culture of his time. And in contrast to what is usually argued, I should like to contend that the famous and often discussed pericopes in the letter to the Romans[1] do not assist us in our evalu-

touches on the central question of this book, which will be dealt with extensively in Chapter Four. Obviously such a question cannot be settled by exegesis alone, because the elucidation of a scriptural text such as this one is influenced by the exegesist's conception of the person and actions of Jesus Christ as a whole. Principles of Biblical theology and theology in general are also at stake, as will be subsequently shown. Discussion of the relation of exegesis to the aforementioned branches of scholarship is irrelevant here.

[1] See *inter alia* H. Kraemer, *Religion and the Christian Faith*, 1956.

ation of the non-Christian religions of the present day. A search in Paul's letters for passages where he has something to say about the Gentiles brings to light Rom. 1.18—32; 2.1—24 and 3.29, 30. But what, strictly speaking, is the tenor of these pericopes? In Rom. 1.18-32 Paul censures the godlessness and injustice of people who, although they know God by the things He has made, have surrendered themselves to the worship of images. The characterization is given only in general terms. The term 'gentile' does not occur here. The statement that the people whom Paul is accusing know God in the things He has made—words in which with some difficulty one can read the doctrine of natural or universal revelation—does not present us with a criterion for the evaluation of the quality of the truth contained in existing historical non-Christian religions which seriously claim that their origins are not to be traced to natural revelation but to God having revealed himself to their founders and spiritual leaders. In the pericope Rom. 2.1—24 the most striking verses are fourteen and fifteen where Paul describes Gentiles who without possessing the law do what the law commands by nature and thus are their own law. Here Paul gives evidence of humane broadmindedness and pastoral consciousness. These verses do not have any fundamental significance in connection with Paul's argument in this chapter, since the tenor of the whole passage is that sinners will not escape God's judgement regardless of whether they possess the law or are their own law. Rom. 3.28—30 is linked up with this: man is only justified by his faith and not by his success in keeping the law. Salvation can be granted to the circumcised and uncircumcised alike. Thus one is obliged to conclude that the problem of the relationship between the gospel and non-Christian religion lay beyond the theological horizon of the Pauline letters.

Such a negative conclusion would at first sight appear alarming. To avoid misunderstanding as to its scope, it should be emphasized that such an inference in no way deprives the Gospels and Paul's letters of their authority in the central questions of the Christian faith. In matters concerning the relation between man and God and man and his fellows and the fundamental commandments of justice, love and peacefulness, Jesus and Paul speak plain language which should be binding for every Christian. But the complex questions concerning our evaluation of culture and the relation between Christianity and the non-Christian religions lay beyond their ken. Hence it is a vain task to try and distill advice in these matters from the *letter* of the Gospels or the Pauline epistles.

Yet Paul must have been capable of throwing light on these questions. His sermon on the Areopagus is in my opinion proof of this. In Athens Paul was obliged to change his strategy. This was after all the first encounter between the gospel and autonomous Greek culture. A man of Christ, a theologian, who changes his strategy finds himself saying things he has not said before, without necessarily repudiating his unspoken conviction. For Paul in Athens there was no reason to preach Christology or justification by faith alone. There were other questions at stake.

INTENTIONAL EXEGESIS

To gain insight into the meaning that Acts 17 has for us today a particular type of exegesis in required: one which is intentional rather than verbal. These terms may need some explanation. By verbal exegesis is meant the impartial and painstaking study of the Scriptures which proceeds from the question: What is written in the Bible and how should these scriptural words be understood? As the only reliable basis for historical research both into the meaning of the texts made use of by the historian of religions and in Bible studies, it warrants our respect and esteem. The Christian theologian has, however, a dual relationship to the Bible: on the one hand the Old and New Testaments are for him objects of unbiased, strictly scientific inquiry, on the other these books contain God's message which possesses for him absolute authority. In the word of the text may be heard the Word of God. But not every letter attests to God's spirit. Hence the task is to extract the kerygma from the written text. Although verbal exegesis is an indispensable first step towards ascertaining the kerygma, alone it cannot lead us to an understanding of what the gospel has to say to us today. On the contrary, it sometimes leads to a kind of neo-Biblicism, as a result of which the essence of Christianity is believed to have been formulated if the ideas of the evangelists, of Paul and of the other letter-writers have been faithfully reproduced. But those who merely repeat what is written in the Bible are not comprehensible to the present generation, and they delude themselves if they think that they are conveying the kerygma. To bring the gospel to life in our time an intentional exegesis is required, that is, an exegesis which seeks the purport of the pericopes and the principal themes of the Biblical proclamation. This is especially true for the solution of problems that lay beyond the scope of the Biblical writers. Here what Troeltsch has to say about 'eine christlich-soziale Bemeisterung der Lage' is *mutatis mutandis* extremely applicable: 'hier werden neue Gedanken nötig sein, ...sie werden aus der inneren Triebkraft der christlichen Idee und ihrer lebendig-gegenwärtigen Neugestaltung herausgeholt werden müssen.'[1]

Intentional exegesis! Perhaps it will be suggested that verbal exegesis is also intentional in so far as it

[1] E. Troeltsch, *Die Soziallehren der christlichen Kirchen und Gruppen*, 1912, p. 985.

seeks the meaning of the written word. This, of course, is true, and so it is desirable to elucidate further the nature of intentional exegesis as we understand it here. Intentional exegesis is the search for the evangelical motifs underlying particular parts of the Bible. It is based on the assumption that the Biblical kerygma possesses a specific structure, in the same way that every religion is a spiritual edifice in which a certain religious logic is developed. To give an example, the basic pattern of every religion is determined by the union between three factors, namely, God, man and religion in the sense of the cult and the carrying out of God's will in man's personal life.[1] Only by study and personal faith in the Bible can one become acquainted with the structure of the Biblical kerygma. One then discovers that the structure of the Biblical kerygma is determined by particular motifs. These motifs lie concealed beneath the literal text and cannot always be expressed precisely by such and such a Biblical word, especially when it is a question of an evangelical evaluation of an issue that was not of primary importance in Jesus' day.

H. de Vos has adopted this line in his book *Het Christendom en de andere godsdiensten*. De Vos is fully alive to the fact that, strictly speaking, his attitude towards his subject cannot be justified Biblically. And so, as he says himself, he has taken a bold leap and

[1] C. J. Bleeker, *De structuur van de godsdienst*, n.d.

'instead of starting out from a few texts and passages in the Bible he has chosen as his point of departure the Biblical kerygma in its entirety'.[1] This simply means that in solving certain problems one allows oneself to be guided by one of the basic motifs of the evangelical proclamation. A theoretical justification for intentional exegesis, which is intended to uncover these motifs, has been provided by A. Nygren in the introductory chapters to his study of Eros and Agape.[2] Nygren argues that religio-historical and theological scholarship should pay greater attention to fundamental concepts which supply the driving force in certain forms of religion. He calls this the investigation of motifs. He defends himself against the allegation that such an investigation might well be arbitrary with two arguments. First, he points out that one does not assure oneself of objectivity simply by confining oneself to separate facts (in this case to the letter of certain texts), since this method of working leads to an intellectual atomism which does not approach spiritual reality; secondly, it would be wrong to suppose that the investigation of motifs relies primarily on uncontrollable intuition. Admittedly, intuition blazes the trail. But its findings must be tested scientifically. Nygren believes that the motif can be

[1] H. de Vos, *op. cit.*, 1962, pp. 123-4.
[2] A. Nygren, *Den Kristna Kärlekstanken genom tiderna* (Eros och Agape), 3rd ed. 1947, part I, introduction.

verified by objective tests. For as soon as it is removed from the religion in question, the latter loses its cohesion. An example of an attempt to formulate the evangelical motifs may be found in G. J. Heering's description of 'the principal features of the Christian faith according to the New Testament'.[1] This is an interesting outline of the motifs on which the kerygma is based.

Intentional exegesis is not a theological pastime but an urgent requirement of our day. Our generation is living in great times, in which the emergence of new nations and enormous changes in the structure of society are taking place at a breathtaking rate, quite apart from the astonishing achievements with which science confronts us time and time again. Statesmen possess the courage to take radical decisions. World events move forward relentlessly. Christians must not lag behind. In fact they should surpass the secular world in imaginative power, in acuteness of vision, in the finding of new paths. In particular, they should resolutely endeavour to clear up a number of extremely important problems which they have discussed endlessly without ever reaching a final decision. The problems I am referring to are those dealt with in this book, namely those relating to the definition of the Christian attitude towards modern culture and the non-Christian religions.

[1] G. J. Heering, *Geloof en openbaring* II, 1937, p. 74 ff.

To avoid misunderstanding it is desirable to make a few comments on the degree of theological importance that may be attributed to these questions. It goes without saying that the heart of Christian theology lies elsewhere, namely in the relationship between man and God and man and his fellowmen. One can, if one wishes, accord only a peripheral significance to the problems which are raised here and which are frequently considered to be a matter for the intellect rather than for the faithful heart. But then it should be realized that everything that takes place on the periphery has a direct influence on the inner parts. This does not only apply to the human body in which every superficial sensation is instantly conveyed to the consciousness, it also applies to Christianity as the *corpus Christi*. The confrontation with modern culture and the non-Christian religions which takes place on the fringes of the Christian religious consciousness and theological concerns will, if it is taken seriously, have immediate repercussions on one's view of Christianity. For an intensive study of the questions raised must inevitably lead to a new attempt to formulate what the gospel has to say to us today. An interaction is brought into play. Anyone who seriously asks himself what his attitude as a Christian should be in these times, is thrown back upon himself as a Christian. He will wonder: What has Christ to say to me and my contemporaries in this modern Athens?

Such a question always leads back to the Bible, because the Christian seeks an attitude which is evangelically justifiable. In this search intentional exegesis is his only guide.

THREE MOTIFS

For reasons which will be apparent from the above, certain features of Paul's sermon in Acts 17 will not be discussed here, as for example the meaning of the altar-inscription 'To an Unknown God' (v. 23), or the meaning of Paul's statement concerning the descent of the human race in verse 26, questions which are essential in a verbal exegesis. Instead the full emphasis will lie on three motifs which may give us some indication of how we should deal with the problems at hand. For this our attention will be directed towards three specific passages. In order to make it clear that we are concerned solely with evangelical motifs, and that it does not matter whether or not the historical Paul expressed himself exactly in this fashion, his name will be placed between inverted commas, whenever the sermon is quoted.

The passages referred to are the following:

(1) Verse 28 where 'Paul' quotes a phrase that is generally attributed to the poet Aratus: 'We are also his offspring.' This is a further explanation of his statement that God 'is not far from each one of us', so

that 'in him we live and move, in him we exist'. The question whether Paul really can have said this is not important here. The accent should be placed on the fact that with this quotation 'Paul' acknowledges the significance of Greek culture.

(2) Verse 22 where the apostle says to the Athenians: 'I see that in everything that concerns religion you are uncommonly scrupulous.' To doubt the veracity of these words is to brand the apostle a cunning politician or equivocator. In the mouth of a courageous and broadminded man like Paul, who was a convinced adherent of Jesus Christ, these words can only be a declaration of his respect for the other religions and an acknowledgement of the quality of their truth.

(3) Verses 30—31 where 'Paul' calls for repentance, alluding at the same time to Jesus Christ who was sent by God, raised from the dead and chosen to judge the world. Here a purely evangelical motif is sounded, as witness Jesus' appeal: 'repent, and believe the gospel' (Mark 1.15). In these words Paul disclosed to the Athenians the motif that gives to Christianity its unique character.

These three motifs, when linked together, are the foundations on which the theme of this book *Christ in Modern Athens* stands. By modern Athens is meant present-day Western-European culture which has to a large extent sprung from the free thinking to which ancient Athens gave birth. This is the setting in which the confrontation, referred to in the sub-title of this book, takes place. And the first question we are prompted to ask is: What does Christ mean in modern Athens?

CHRIST IN MODERN ATHENS

The religious imagination has often been gripped by the question of what would happen if Jesus were to return to earth, not as the awaited judge of mankind or as the ruler of God's Kingdom finally about to be established on earth, but as a preacher as he once was in Galilee. What would he say? How would he react to the behaviour of twentieth-century man and to present-day society? Imaginative writers have even ventured to depict his appearance in our world, but they could have saved themselves the trouble of giving shape to this hypothetical possiblility. For Christ lives in our midst; he is to be found in modern Athens. Kierkegaard has rightly claimed that a true relationship towards Jesus can only be achieved if we look upon him not as an historical figure but as a contemporary.[1] Or to put it differently: he comes to us across the centuries and makes an appeal to believers and unbelievers alike. A depiction of a Quaker meeting given as a frontispiece to J. W. Harvey Theobald's book on Quakerism illustrates this truth very vividly.

[1] S. Kierkegaard, *Einübung im Christentum* (*Gesammelte Werke* 26, 1955) p. 63: "und da Christus das Unbedingte ist, sieht man leicht, dass es im Verhältnis zu ihm nur eine Lage gibt: die Gleichzeitigkeit."

It is entitled: The Presence in the Midst. Men and women are sitting together silently, listening with an inner ear, seeing with an inner eye. For in their midst Christ, a spiritual reality, is preaching to them.[1]

The discovery that Christ is present in our century brings about a repetition of the original situation, described in the Gospels of Matthew and Mark (Matt. 4.18—20; Mark 1.16—18). He suddenly confronts us without our knowing where he comes from and who he really is, and he calls to us to follow him. The first thing that anyone who has recognized Christ's presence today hears is the time-honoured exhortation: "Repent, and believe the Gospel" (Matt. 4.17; Mark 1.15). Paul alludes to this summons when he says in his sermon on the Areopagus that God "commands mankind, all men everywhere, to repent" (Acts 17.30). This is a clear reference to the central theme of the proclamation of Jesus of Nazareth. Some exegetists refuse to see in the great apostle to the Gentiles' Athenian sermon a proclamation of the gospel of Christ, because it does not contain any Christological references. If, however, it is borne in mind that, as Matt. 4 and Mark 1 tell us, Simon Peter and Andrew were not required to make any formal confession of their faith in Christ, but that their immediate willingness to follow Jesus was sufficient to make disciples of them, then it is plain enough that the sermon on the

[1] J. W. Harvey Theobald, *Quakerism, a plain statement*, 1931.

Areopagus is a true albeit implicit proclamation of the gospel.

For nineteen centuries Christian theologians have struggled with the Christological problem of who Jesus of Nazareth was and what his relation was to God. The amount of thought that famous theologians have given to the solution of this problem is impressive. Creeds through the ages bear an eloquent testimony to this fact. They contain Christological definitions which are interesting attempts to formulate the religious significance of Jesus Christ. These definitions have retained much of value, even though a modern Christian cannot concur with them entirely; for every age must make its own evaluation of the figure of Christ. Some observations on this subject will be given in a later chapter. Here it may be useful to remark that a clear distinction should be made between belief in Christ and Christology, although no one will deny that the two are extremely closely connected. This chapter is devoted to the question: What does Christ mean today to true Christians? Hence for the three following reasons Christological considerations will not be entered into here.[1] First, a Christology that does not express the belief in Christ of a par-

[1] For the same reason no survey will be given of the many, complex new testamentary and dogmatic problems attendant upon Christology. Neither has it been deemed necessary to include a list of the relevant literature, which would be bound to be incomplete.

ticular time will obscure the significance of Jesus rather than clarify it. Secondly, no Christology has ever wholly captured the secret of the essential nature of Jesus Christ, so that there is none to which absolute authority may be ascribed. Thirdly, only in faith can we understand who he is, in the same direct way in which the first disciples understood who he was and what he wanted when he suddenly appeared beside their fishingboats by the Sea of Galilee.

Thanks to the Gospels Christ is revealed to present-day Christendom as an impressive figure. He appears in modern Athens as a person of authority. To be sure, the Gospels and Paul's letters in particular contain the germs of Christological definitions which can sometimes create difficulties for twentieth-century Christians. Nevertheless, the Gospels always remain true to their missionary nature. They are not a repository of theological treatises but of a proclamation which is called the gospel, because it brings the good news of the revelation of God's holy love in the person and message of Jesus Christ. The bringer of this message is portrayed so vividly, so directly and so strikingly than even though we possess neither a biography nor a description of his appearance, no one who reads the New Testament thoughtfully can escape the powerful influence he radiates. In Christ the reader encounters a divine messenger who not only made an overpowering impression on his contemporaries—does not the Bible testify to the power with which he preached?—but who still today casts a spell over those who have heard his message, whether willingly or not.

What strikes the reader of the Gospels most deeply and commands his respect is that he becomes aquainted with a man who is truly human because not only does he proclaim the great religious truths, with love in the vanguard, but he also practises them in daily life. His care of the sick and mentally ill, his association with sinners and outcasts, his suffering and death al testify to this.

That the Gospels conclude with accounts of Jesus' resurrection is not to be wondered at. His disciples could not but be convinced, even though after some hesitation and uncertainty, that the cross and death were unable to destroy him. He was too powerful and hence he had to gain the victory over hatred and death. This is the meaning of the stories of the empty grave and his appearances. Whoever takes the relevant passages literally will become enmeshed in the contradictions which occur in them and will find it difficult to accept the idea of Jesus' resurrection from the dead. These objections are swept away, once one realizes that Christ still makes just as immediate an appeal to us as he did to Simon Peter and Andrew nineteen hundred years ago. Many profound thinkers and bearers of great truths have made themselves heard in the course of human history. Their writings are respected, but the revitalizing impulses which proceed from their words are few. Jesus Christ is unique because he backed up his message with his life. For this reason he is still a living reality today and his words have lost nothing of their power. With his essential nature as mysterious as ever, he moves among us and is to be found in modern Athens.

Jesus of Nazareth, Jesus, Jesus Christ and Christ — we have freely used all these names behind which certain Christological definitions can lie concealed. For our purposes, however, these terms do not need to be thus loaded. Since the Gospels themselves are non-dogmatic in character, we do not, in this chapter, wish to express any views on dogmas such as the incarnation, the two personalities of Christ or the Trinity. Profound though these dogmas may be, they obscure the original significance of Christ, because they are built up of notions which have lost their immediacy for modern man. Here we are concerned with Jesus Christ as he appears to us from the New Testament and the Gospels in particular. In calling him Jesus or Jesus of Nazareth, the emphasis lies on the fact that he lived nineteen hundred years ago. There is no reason to doubt his historicity. Strictly speaking, none of the historical fachts can be verified. So long, however, as statements concerning historical events would seem to be reliable, there is no reason to

doubt their accuracy. This is equally the case with the
Gospels as a source of information on the actions of
Jesus and the origins of Christianity. For a Christian
these statements are not only of historical interest,
but they are also fraught with redemptive meaning.
In Jesus he encounters God's purpose for man. Jesus
of Nazareth has acquired religious significance for his
followers. Whenever his presence is experienced, it is
as the Christ rather than as the rabbi or prophet of
Nazareth. This title was already bestowed upon him
by his disciples to indicate that they looked upon him
as the Saviour, the ruler of the Kingdom of God. In
Paul's vocabulary Christ is for those who believe in
him the Lord transfigured by suffering, death and resurrection. He is a man of light. He is not, however,
merely a conception or a product of the imagination,
since he has his roots in the facts of history. He is a
personal presence who exerts spiritual power.

The significance of Christ in modern Athens is twofold: first, he radiates indisputable authority. Theologians have repeatedly endeavoured to give this
authority a particular Christological basis bij claiming,
for example, that his word possesses authority because he is the only-begotten Son of God, the incarnation of the Word of God. Such dogmatic corner-
stones to Christ's authority are by no means without
their use. Yet they are not convincing to everyone
and moreover they prove nothing. Authority can

never be rationally explained. It is its own mouth-piece and it asserts itself by means of its own strength. A Christian accepts Christ's authority as the revelation of God's sacred love with intuitive certainty and yields to it with the spontaneity of faith. Secondly, with this authority Christ makes a prophetic appeal to man and shows him the way to salvation. When all is said and done the influence that Christ still exerts must be attributed to his ability to inspire and awaken man's faith in him.

Concealed behind this formal description of the present-day meaning of Christ lies the so-called kerygma or message of the New Testament. Obviously, this truth calls for further elucidation. Here, however, we shall not pause to scrutinize the kerygma more fully, since such a scrutiny is only of value if the kerygma is related to the problems and questions of the modern world. The confrontation of the gospel with the cultural and spiritual problems of our century will be dealt with in the following chapters. Our purpose here is to allow the person and teachings of Christ to speak for themselves in all their immediacy. An attempt has already been made to delineate Christ. Now the principal themes of his preaching which is indissolubly linked with his person demands our attention.[1] These themes may be summarized as follows:

[1] The person and preachings of Jesus Christ form a unity in

(1) The gospel is the good news that God, a spiritual and personal being, the only one who deserves our worship and obedience, will in His sacred love have mercy on mankind and the world.

(2) God has revealed Himself and His will, to which the preaching of His messengers has in the course of history borne witness, in the person and proclamation of Jesus, whom his followers have acknowledged as the Christ.

(3) The gospel makes a direct appeal to man: it summons him to come to a decision and to be converted in the knowledge that he may be assured of God's forgiveness of his sins and may hope for the support of the Holy Spirit in his efforts to live a spiritual life.

(4) The imitation of Christ should consist in the performance of deeds of brotherly love and the application of a sense of justice. For God wishes His Kingdom to be established here on earth. In a purely religious sense the notion of God's Kingdom implies a judgement of all earthly events, while it is at the

the New Testament. Hence it is wrong to separate them. On the one hand this is done by those for whom his proclamation alone is the essence of Christianity, on the other by those who claim that the gospel is wholly concentrated in the person of Jesus Christ. But Jesus Christ remains a cipher bringing neither revelation of God nor acting as a mentor in faith, unless his teachings and his life are linked with his person. It is these that give colour and consistency to his person. This question will come up again in Chapter Four.

same time the highest of all spiritual expectations.

This kerygma is in the words of Jesus the fire with which he was to set the world ablaze. It caused spiritual and social explosions and it has as yet lost nothing of its heat. Even today the Christian faith would seem to be best characterized as a perilous truth. The implications of the perilous nature of the evangelical truth will emerge in the course of our investigation.

In this book we do not presume to present a rewording of the Christian faith in its entirety. As has already been remarked, the heart of the Christian faith, namely the relation between God and Man, will not be examined here. We are confining ourselves to a study of the encounter between the gospel and the world of our times. For Christians this subject gives rise to the following questions:

(1) What should our attitude be towards the culture of our time?

(2) How should we evaluate the non-Christian religions?

(3) What may our expectations be as to the future of religion and of Christianity in particular?

These are the three questions that arise from the present-day world-situation, and to which Christians must seek a solution. They are questions which plainly lay beyond the horizon of Jesus and also of Christians in bygone centuries. The New Testament does not therefore offer us any clear-cut directives. The im-

portance of Paul's sermon on the Areopagus is, however, that it does give us some indication of how we
can approach and solve these problems in accordance
with the spirit of the gospel.

THE CHRISTIAN ATTITUDE TOWARDS MODERN CULTURE

Ever since Paul visited Athens and debated with the philosophers of his day, Christianity has wrestled with the problem of its relation to the culture around it. The issue has presented itself in a variety of forms through the ages and has never been settled satisfactorily. The very nature of the gospel well nigh excludes the possibility of true harmony between Christianity and culture. The truth that Jesus proclaimed is derived from a higher sphere and is not palatable to a society in which self-interest and expediency are the order of the day. The world does not wish to accept this truth. And for those who tend to forget this hard fact, the cross at Golgotha is there to serve as a constant reminder. Nevertheless, the Good News that Jesus proclaimed was intended for this earthly existence. In order to attain salvation mankind and society must heed this message. The absolute truth of the gospel cannot be modified to suit the relativity of human society. The moment Christianity allies itself too closely to worldly norms, it loses its purity and grandeur. If, on the other hand, it keeps aloof from the culture around it, it will fail to be effective. The history of the Church is a fascinating record of how in the course of the centuries Christianity has oscillated between adapting itself to and remaining aloof from the culture around it.

The first Christians who anticipated the second coming of the Lord would have no truck with the culture of their time. When the Christian Church became the state church, it had to reconcile itself to the worldly order. Christianity never obtained a firm hold on Hellenistic culture. The Middle Ages, however, saw the birth of a mighty synthesis between the truth of the gospel and the cultural life of the time, a synthesis which could be justified both theologically and socially. Even so voices were raised, which protested in the name of the gospel against a unity that was illusionary. In the Renaissance the purely Christian culture began to show the first signs of dissolution. The various fields of culture, science, arts and government regained their independence. The secularization of communal life began to take shape. This autonomous culture demanded a fresh approach on the part of Christian thinkers. The familiar story was repeated: on the one hand enthusiastic attempts were made to bridge the gap between Christianity and culture; on the other the old Christian distrust of a depraved world was once more aroused. This bird's-eye view of the historical development is sufficient here, as the subject has repeatedly been dealt with in an examplary manner by capable scholars. Neither is there any lack of analyses describing the course of European cultural history since the Renaissance.[1]

Our immediate concern in this chapter is the contemporary Christian attitude towards modern culture. The urgency of this problem is brought home to us by the three following considerations. Firstly, it may be observed that Christianity does not retire from the world as a matter of principle, it is not hostile to culture but critical of it. The Christian attitude to the world is positive rather than negative. For one of the pillars of Christianity is the belief, founded on Genesis I, that God has created this world and that it is therefore good; even though the Christian must acknowledge to his bewilderment that sin has inexplicably corrupted God's creation. A comparison with the way in which Indian religions contemplate the world illuminates the Christian outlook on temporal affairs. These religons ascribe no *telos* or purpose to the world: the universe undergoes a never-ending process of periodic destruction and rebirth; by good works, true insight or belief in a saviour-god man must free himself from his attachment to this deceptive earthly life and thus endeavour to escape the cycle of rebirths. These religions do not have a fundamentally positive attitude towards the culture around them, despite the fact that many of their adherents relish the joys of earthly life, and although in more recent times attempt

[1] For example the works of E. Troeltsch and M. Weber.

have been made to find a socio-ethically justified approach to urgent social problems.[1] As Christianity, in contrast to the Indian religions, is founded on a belief in creation, it is constantly forced to define its attitude towards culture. A basic problem presents itself here. There is no denying that Christianity is by origin critical of culture. Unfortunately this critical sense is sometimes converted into an unmotivated distrust. For this reason it is highly desirable to give fresh thought to this question.

Secondly, we have come to realize that this problem has entered a new phase. Our culture has developed new features which stimulate a reappraisal; or to put it differently, the consequences of certain cultural aspirations have suddenly become so manifest that Christians are obliged to make a re-evaluation of their attitude.

Thirdly, it should be borne in mind that Christianity cannot sanctify the world, as is its mission, unless it finds the words and attitude that will make it comprehensible and acceptable to this generation. Christianity can only make an impression and have an influence in the world today if it assumes a form that is both distinctively Christian and culturally acceptable. The problem of the Christian attitude to modern culture is therefore closely linked with the burning

[1] A. Schweitzer, *Die Weltanschauung der Indischen Denker, Mystik und Ethik*, 1935.

question of the way the gospel should be presented in our day.

Towards a Definition of Culture

The very urgency of the problem is a stimulus for us to define the subject accurately, before we venture to make any pronouncements. The first question to arise is: What is the structure and range of modern culture? Culture is a chameleon-like phenomenon. It is not surprising that it has been approached in a variety of ways. One method of analysis, which has been adopted by the Dutch historian, J. Huizinga, is the historical one.[1] But an historical view, however interesting it may be in itself, does not offer us sufficient enlightenment here, as our concern is with modern culture, which bears its own signature. A more useful starting-point is offered by a general definition such as the following: "Culture is the reality that man himself creates by his actions and places alongside the reality that exists independently of man."[2] This holds for every culture without exception. Culture is a product of the organizing and creative ability of man who uses the forces and possibilities of nature in order to build up a form of existence which

[1] J. Huizinga, *Geschonden wereld, een beschouwing over de kansen op herstel van onze beschaving*, 1945.
[2] *Eerste Nederlandse Systematisch Ingerichte Encyclopaedie* (E.N. S.I.E.) I, p. 147.

enables him to live as a spiritual and intellectual being. In culture man realizes his urge to transcend himself: as a civilized being he rises above his impulses. Hence culture always demands a certain degree of self-discipline. Culture is a blessing, an enrichment of life, but it is also a task, a burden: its preservation demands self-control and the sacrifice of self-indulgence and of the gratification of animal passions.

From this tentative definition it is evident that we would be restricting the range of culture unwarrantedly, if we were only to include in it certain of man's higher intellectual achievements such as art, philosophy and science. Among cultural phenomena are to be reckoned habits and manners, various sports and the many methods of mass-communication, such as the newspaper, radio, television, cinema and theatre. Culture does not merely consist in ideal values, it manifests itself in the material things of life. It finds realization in the many social and humanitarian institutions, and in particular in innumerable technical inventions.

These remarks must serve to clear the way for a more precise description of those facets of modern culture which are at variance with Christianity. A large number of cultural factors may be eliminated. To begin with the term "modern culture" in the sense of a contemporary world-wide culture is so comprehensive that its description would fill many volumes.

It is even debatable whether we may use the word in the singular at all. There are after all in the world at this moment a variety of cultures, as for instance the Indian, Chinese and Japanese, all of which have their own origins and characteristics. Mention is made of them because they each represent imposing and original values. But we are not concerned with them here. By modern culture we mean the typically Western civilization which was born of the inventive thinking of the Greeks and which, since the beginning of our era, has been pervaded by the spirit of Christianity and classical humanism. This culture developed in a spectacular fashion and has clearly demonstrated its boundless energy. Disseminated by enterprising European nations, it conquered the world in the colonial era. All the peoples on earth have breathed and still do breathe the spirit of this remarkable culture. They have grown to know its virtues and vices, its nobility and its corruption. Hence the problems of Western culture are the problems of humanity. Where this is not yet the case, it will be so in due course. This is why we may restrict ourselves exclusively to the problem of Christianity's attitude towards modern culture within the sphere of Western European civilization.

Furthermore, to achieve the sharpest possible focus on the problem in hand, it is necessary to leave a number of facets of this culture undiscussed. Firstly, problems such as the struggle against social injustice and the curtailment of the danger of war will not be touched upon here. Not because they are unimportant in the eyes of a Christian. Quite to the contrary, but they belong rather within the realm of Christian social ethics than to the subject in hand.

Secondly, a number of cultural manifestations, such as sport, the products of the mass-media and the arts are of little relevance here. To be sure, Christianity should at some time state where it stands with respect to such cultural phenomena, but they have no fundamental and independent bearing on the question at hand since they can be traced to more deeply seated aspirations which determine the structure of our culture. The reader may well express surprise at the exclusion of the arts from such a confrontation. This is not to disparage their achievement. No one can deny that the arts act as a highly sensitive gauge to imminent cultural changes. But it is precisely as such that they are a mouthpiece of certain propulsive cultural factors rather than that these arise from the arts. Hence the arts are subordinated to the cultural tendencies which concern us here.

Thirdly, modern culture displays certain features and tendencies, which may not be left unmentioned, but which are of no immediate interest here. It goes without saying that depravity and want of principle are extensive in modern culture. At every step habits may be observed of which no one with any moral or religious scruples can approve. It is sometimes difficult not to be vexed at the immaturity and lack of taste that abound in our society. Such symptoms of cultural decadence are alarming, but they do not diminish the value of the notions upon which modern culture is built. A more serious matter is the rapidly increasing secularization and desecration of various traditonally Christian institutions. For this is a direct threat to Christianity, since the Christian faith and the Christian Church are thus deprived of certain of their functions. In some religious circles it has in fact become *bon ton* to refer to the time we live in as "post-Christian", to condemn outright modern culture with its so-called satanic features and to depict the prospects for the future in the darkest colours. Such a condemnation is not only unfair and thoughtless, but also vastly exaggerated. Nobody that has had any acquaintance with cultures that have not fallen under the influence of Christianity, as for intsance Islam, despairs of the continued existence of Western European culture, so long as the Greek thirst for truth and the Christian *caritas* prevail. Indeed, on closer examination, the phenomenon of growing secularization is so complex that we should not judge it too rashly. Dechristianization and decreases in church-membership are not wholly detrimental; they can also mean a purification of Christendom. Furthermore, the spiritual content of certain cultural manifestations is sometimes underestimated. The sacred presents itself in new guises. There are, for example, works of art, not inspired by Biblical or religious motifs, which nevertheless display a deeply religious spirit. The whole problem of secularization has so many facets that it would only confuse the issue to deal with it here.

Lastly, no attention will be paid to all manner of popular speculations on the spirit and personality of twentieth-century man, on his isolation and insecurity.[1] However much truth there may be in cultural analyses of this kind, and however sharp and absorbing they may be, they only possess ephemeral value. What is written today on this subject is out-of-date tomorrow. Here we are interested in the enduring characteristics and pathos of the modern cultural pattern.

Having stated our reasons for passing over all these aspects so lightly, we may now turn to the principal incentives of modern culture. Proceeding from the definition of culture as "the reality which man himself creates by his actions" we may postulate that our culture is at present dominated by the desire to harness natural forces by means of bold scientific investigation and unsurpassed technological skill.

---

[1] See for example A. Weber, *Der dritte und der vierte Mensch*, 1953; H. Szczesny, *Die Zukunft des Unglaubens*, 1958.

Triumphs of the Intellect

In some fields of human endeavour man's creative
ability long ago reached heights that can scarcely be
surpassed today. Art and philosophy are striking examples of this. The prehistoric cave-paintings testify
to an artistic vision and skill which are little short of
astounding, if we recall that these works were created
by people who could not boast of any culture in the
traditional sense of the word. In philosophy and ethics
the ancient Greeks gave so much thought to fundamental questions that their formulations still possess
prototypical value. In one field, however, the ancients
were mere beginners, namely in the natural sciences
and technology.[1] Yet we would be doing them an
injustice if we were to deny that they practised a type
of science that warrants our respect and admiration.
Nevertheless, this was as the Dutch historian of religion, W. B. Kristensen, has clearly shown not
science in the modern sense of the word, but a search
for wisdom which would give man insight into the
mystery of life and death and thus guarantee his virtue
and happiness.[2] Science as we know it today is derived
from the free and critical thinking of the ancient
Greeks. When what Jacob Burckhardt calls "the dis-

[1] R. J. Forbes, *Man, the Maker, A History of Technology and
Engineering*, 1950.
[2] W. B. Kristensen, *The Meaning of Religion*, 1960.

covery of the world and of man"[1] took place in the Renaissance, that is to say when man discovered the power of his intellect and began to appreciate the goods of the earth, there awoke in his heart an insatiable longing to understand and dominate nature. It was then that he embarked upon the scientific adventure which has led to so many triumphs of the intellect. With the torch of reasoning man penetrates ever deeper into the darkness of the unknown. In the footsteps of the scholars have followed the technologists who convert the discoveries of the former into appliances and apparatuses with which numerous practical problems have been solved or which have increased the well-being and comfort of mankind considerably.

There is no need for us to trace the history of the natural sciences or to give a survey of the problems arising from their development, assuming always that we would be capable of doing so. Suffice to say that empirical reasoning has given physicists, chemists, physicians, psychologists, psychiatrists, and economists an ever firmer grasp on the object of their investigations. With highly refined apparatus the secrets of the microcosm and the macrocosm are fathomed. A detailed description of these scientific activities would only lead us further away from our problem. A single example is sufficient to illustrate the pathos, charac-

[1] J. Burckhardt, *The Civilization of the Renaissance in Italy*, II.

teristics and consequences of the dilemma in which these triumphs of the intellect have placed us.

The example we have in mind is the computer.[1] For to our surprise and dismay we are discovering that the principles of automation have far more wide-reaching application than was previously thought possible. Indeed, experts predict that the computer will bring about not only an industrial revolution but also a cultural one. The advent of the computer on the cultural scene means that this robot is also involved in the problem of the confrontation of Christianity with modern culture. It may be remarked in passing that this involvement is the justification for the prominent position which—possibly to the bewilderment of some readers—has been given in this chapter to the dominance of science and technology in modern culture. For it is on this front that the battle for the future structure of our culture is being fought. The computer proves this. This ingenious machine not only solves mathematical problems at an incredible speed and with unfailing accuracy, but it can also be put to use in translating, the processing of data and in drawing conclusions from the information it receives. The computer has a memory, can correct itself, think and make decisions quicker and more accurately than the human brain. The number of possible

[1] Prof. E. H. P. Baudet and others, *Mens en Computer, automatie, industriële en culturele revolutie*, 1963.

applications for the principle of automation is im-
mense. The computer is already a force to be reckoned
with in various sectors of life, including the world of
politics. It is for instance not widely known that during
the Korean war President Truman ruled that General
MacArthur should not cross the Yalu river because
according to a computer China would then declare
war on America. Thereupon MacArthur resigned his
commission.[1] This speaks volumes. Not much imagination is called for to envisage how the computer can
similarly influence the course of our cultural life, even
though it is clear that great discoveries in the fields
of science and the arts will remain the privilege of
genius, compared with which the computer is only a
stupid robot. But the number of geniuses is small and
culture is propagated by the mass of ordinary people,
over whom the computer could easily acquire as-
cendancy.

The computer is testimony to the pathos of the
development of science and technology. Spurred on
by an inner logic the intellect continually tries to
penetrate ever further into the secrets of nature in
order to apply the knowledge it obtains in the exe-
cution of breathtaking technological feats. This endeavour is inevitable and cannot be halted. The clock
of history cannot be turned back. It is for instance
impossible to divest ourselves of our knowledge of

[1] *Ibid.*, p. 141.

atomic energy. This state of affairs entails dangers, which we cannot afford to ignore. J. R. Oppenheimer, the famous physicist, knew what he was talking about when he wrote: "Even in pure science, with no thoughts of practice, no weapons, no bombs, no immediate change in human life, a great discovery is a source of terror". And he goes on to recall what Niels Bohr had once said to him: "When I have a great idea, I am always close to suicide."[1] New discoveries, great ideas can be beneficial, but they also possess an explosive force, the range and effect of which no one knows, not even the discoverer. Yet there is no way back. Oppenheimer rightly says: "In science progress is the inevitable consequence of life, of activity". Fortunately this development is not the result of the incessantly curious intellect alone. It is also inspired by what Oppenheimer calls "dedication to improving life on this earth". Culture has always been one of man's weapons in his struggle for existence. Inspired by humanistic motives man today is waging a war for improved living conditions for all the peoples of the earth, a battle against poverty, hunger, disease and ignorance, a battle for greater prosperity, for spiritual freedom, for a truly human existence for the whole of mankind. In this struggle for civilization science and technology are powerful and beneficial weapons.

[1] J. R. Oppenheimer, "The Future of Civilization in the Scientific Age", *France Asie*, Vol. XVII, No. 166, p. 1808.

From the above the characteristics of modern culture may easily be inferred. Its restlessness and dynamism are its most prominent features. In this it differs from ancient cultures. The ancients' conception of the world was static: they had an unquestioning belief in existence and in the validity of a cosmic order ordained at the time of creation, and firmly upheld despite occasional violations. This divine order extended to all fields of life, not only in nature, but also in the realms of culture such as the arts, science, government, ethics, religion and divine worship in particular.[1] Modern culture is fragmentary and chaotic, because the various cultural activities have become autonomous. Furthermore it is constantly changing without there being any indication of where this restless turmoil is leading. Another characteristic is the "anti-magic tendency".[2] That is to say that although contemporary man allows himself to be guided more by irrational impulses than by reason, and even though superstition is still rife, the dominant tone is one of cool reason. In scientific investigation and technological activities the possibility of mysterious magic forces is excluded. The effect of all manipulations is believed to be calculable. In this, mathematics play a leading part as a trustworthy guide. Nature may have her secrets, but she is

[1] C. J. Bleeker, "The Pattern of the Ancient Egyptian Culture" (*Numen* Vol. XI Fasc. 1).
[2] G. Carlberg, *Kultur och Religion*, 1951.

reasonable and yields an answer to every well-formu-
lated question. From this it may be concluded that the
prevailing climate of thought is humanistic in two
meanings of the word. Firstly, because only those data
are accepted as being correct which can be verified
empirically. The general trend of thought is anti-
metaphysical, in other words, the existence of a reality
beyond the perceptible horizon is denied. This attitude
is also shared by the philosophers. Their approach
to problems and the questions they ask are often
closely linked to the methods and observations of the
natural scientists.[1] And it cannot be fortuitous that, as
is the case in phenomenology and existentialism, man
is the centre from which their thoughts proceed.
Secondly, our society is humanistic in the best sense
of the word, in that the value of all cultural activities
is determined by their ability to raise the standard of
human welfare. A further characteristic of modern
culture is that the attention which our technological
achievements demand has made contemporary man
highly other-directed. His interest is especially focussed upon the many things that can enrich his life, not
to speak of the reverse of the coin: his unrestrained
lust for possession and enjoyment. As a result his inner
life is in danger of becoming impoverished. This
orientation towards the material goods of culture can
deprive man of his visionary abilities and his enthu-

[1] C. F. van Weissäcker, *Zum Weltbild der Physik*, 1958.

siasm for idealistic aims. Finally, it is clear that scientific and technological progress is a stern taskmaster. It constantly raises the tempo of work and life, not only in the fields of science and technology, but surprising though it may seem in business, the arts and sport. The business man, the athlete and the artist are required to reach ever higher standards of achievement. The struggle for survival is a bitter one. This fosters a harsh climate and ruthless morality. Civilization has never been a paradise as some starry-eyed idealists believe. It has always been a blessing and a burden. The vehement nature of modern culture makes man's status precarious and ambiguous.

The Christian Attitude towards Modern Culture

In his sermon on the Areopagus Paul quoted from Greek literature to lend his words added force. This gesture, however slight in itself, is in its kind unique in the New Testament. Nowhere else is a clear confrontation with the culture of the time to be found. This deed of Paul's therefore acquires a significance that rises far above that of a casual quotation. By his action Paul acknowledges the value of the Greek culture of his day. This acknowledgement should spur present-day Christians on to adopting an attitude to modern culture, which though critical is fundamentally positive and evangelically justified.

For a Christian there is much to criticize in modern culture. Hence it is only just that he should first pay homage to the fabulously clever work which is being done in science, technology, commerce and industry by highly gifted intellectuals. It must be admitted that what is being achieved under the goad of competition has positive value in so far as it increases the material and mental welfare of humanity. If we are to be objective it is in addition necessary for us to realize that science and technology are basically impartial towards religion. It is pointless to accuse science of arrogance and to claim that it is man-centred as some theologians do. This is an accusation that is also frequently levelled at philosophy. It is a misrepresentation to maintain that science and philosophy by trusting implicitly in reason build a tower of Babel and assault heaven in a sinful passion to glorify man. No scientist or philosopher will understand what is meant by this. For they do nothing but make use of the powers of intellect and reasoning that God has given to man in order that he may uphold himself as a civilized being. The true seeker for knowledge is no Titan but a modest worker who is often deceived in the course of his quest, who is prepared to give up every theory for the sake of a better one, and who now and then experiences the humble joy of being able to satisfy with his work his "sense of order, of beauty, of importance".[1] To

[1] Oppenheimer, *Op. cit.*, p. 1813.

be sure, natural scientists are in the main neo-posi-tivistic in approach.[2] Yet we cannot object to this from a religious point of view, so long as science re-mains true to its empirical principle. What is danger-ous and questionable, however, are the anti- or a-re-ligious world-view and principles which some persons believe they are justified in deducing from their stu-dies. For here the scientist oversteps the bounds of his competence by making a value judgement. A third consideration which we are apt to overlook is that Christians possess no alternative to modern culture. Christians sometimes speak slightingly about modern culture, forgetting meanwhile that it is thanks to this despised Western European culture founded on de-mocratic principles that they enjoy religious freedom and may even air their forthright criticism. This aversion to our culture occasionally smacks of hy-pocrisy because for all his distaste the critic profits freely from all that the culture has to offer. Everyone is at liberty to voice his criticism. But it is foolish to want to saw off the branch on which one is seated.

Now that we have acknowledged the positive assets of modern culture, we may present our own criticism. It will not be gentle. Numerous manifestations of our culture, which have already been referred to in the previous section, provoke our disapproval. It is not

[1] *Philosophy for the Future, The Quest for Modern Materialism,* ed. Roy Wood Sellars, V. J. McGill, Marvin Farber, 1949.

hard to take exception to the abundant lack of taste
displayed almost everywhere or to deplore the absurd
experiments which are made, say, in connection with
the space-projects. More disturbing are the "demoniac" tendencies in modern culture; "demoniac" being
understood in Tillich's sense of "gestaltwidriges
Hervorbrechen des schöpferischen Grundes in den
Dingen".[1] Discoveries have been made, the beneficial
nature of which can be transformed at any moment
into a destructive one. Culture is a double-edged
sword.

The Christian attitude towards modern culture is
highly ambivalent. A Christian lives in this world but
he may not be of this world. He will have to practise
the "innerweltliche Askese", which is according to
E. Troeltsch the predominant characteristic of Cal-
cinism.[2] This means that he consciously accepts modern culture with its scientific and technical orientation
and adapts himself to its climate of thought, because
this is the atmosphere in which his faith must become
a living reality. The Christian will furthermore acknowledge that the dispassionateness and relentless
honesty characteristic of modern man can exert a
purifying influence on his religious life. These qualities are a constant reminder for him to cast his faith

[1] P. Tillich, *Das Dämonische, ein Beitrag zur Sinndeutung der
Geschichte*, 1926.
[2] E. Troeltsch, *Die Soziallehren der Christlichen Kirchen und
Gruppen*, 1912, part two.

in forms that can stand up to the test of human and religious veracity. Anyone who pursues this line of thought is confronted with the problem—alluded to in the previous section—of the guise in which Christianity should appear in this age. In our final chapter on the future of religion this question will be dealt with more fully. Here a few guiding lines will suffice. The Christian who wishes to be heard in this century will have to discard outdated patterns of religious thinking He will even have to reformulate notions that are at the very heart of the message of the gospel, such as the conception of the Kingdom of God. He must show understanding for the complexities of contemporary man's spiritual life and he will have to grasp the fact that many persons are agnostic and sceptical by conviction and that the likelihood of winning them for the gospel is greatest if no attempts are made to convert them.

So on the one hand the Christian feels himself to be highly involved in modern culture, because it is a valuable asset and a wonderful creation of the human spirit. On the other he maintains an inner aloofness from it; for evangelical truth is vastly different from the mores and norms of the world. The Christian knows that there are needs which cannot be alleviated by any of the many boons of culture. In the real crises of life culture is of no avail. The strength to bear suffering, to look death in the eye, must be drawn from another source than that of culture. Man's sense of guilt, his fear of an uncertain future and of the clouding of the intellect can only be overcome if he believes in the prospect of eternity. Culture is a great boon, but it is not an eternal one.[1] Jesus has said, man cannot live by bread alone. The Christian believes in and anticipates a boon which will transcend all the earthly ones. The expectation is bound up with the Kingdom of God, that dimension of the Christian faith which holds in judgement all that happens on earth and at the same time gives meaning to it.

The Church is a representative of this totally different dimension. The contrast between the intrinsic nature of the Church and that of cultural development is striking. Culture proves its value and its right to exist only by what it continually produces, by its unremitting activity. The Church exists not by virtue of its deeds but by its being. It can defy the passing of the centuries, the disfavour of the times and the criticism of mankind; for it arose on the day of the Pentacost when the disciples were filled with the Holy Spirit. Because God made it into a mouthpiece of His Holy Spirit, the Church still testifies to a truth that is everlasting. And so the Christian with his spiritual eye fixed on eternity can show appreciation for modern culture without conforming to the world or losing his powers of discrimination.

[1] H. T. de Graaf, *Om het hoogste goed*, 1918; *Om het eeuwige goed*, 1923.

THE CHRISTIAN EVALUATION OF THE
NON-CHRISTIAN RELIGIONS

In Acts 17.22 Paul says to the Athenians: "I see that in everything that concerns religion you are uncommonly scrupulous." As has already been remarked in Chapter One this statement implies a positive evaluation of non-Christian religious beliefs. Thus Paul indicates the direction in which the solution of the problem of the relation of Christianity to the non-Christian religions must be sought.

Since Paul's days, however, much has changed in this respect. Not only has the horizon of the history of religions been immeasurably broadened, but the problem has become far more pointed, so that it is today one of the issues that determine the position of Christianity in the world. The vast amount of literature on this subject is not to be wondered at. But, to my mind, none of the writers, despite their erudition and keenness of intellect, has succeeded in opening a new and satisfactory vista to this problem. Evidently they lack the courage to grasp the bull by the horns and seek a drastic solution. It would appear that Christian theologians could in this respect learn a thing or two from the far-sighted politicians among their contemporaries. In politics far-reaching decisions are taken, although they are not popular and even unpleasant, because the future welfare of a country or sometimes of the world depends upon them. Theologians should by rights display greater vision than statesmen.

To come to a thorough understanding of the problem we must first have a detailed knowledge of the subject, and secondly, the question itself must be formulated as clearly as possible. Our evaluation will therefore be preceded by a brief summary of the principal historical insights and a precise delineation of the actual problem. The following sections will be devoted to these two points.

A. Historical Insights

The history of religions is a relatively young science which has achieved surprisingly much in the course of its brief existence. True, mankind has always shown interest in its religious past. Even the writings of the ancient historians such as Herodotus (5th century B.C.) contained information on the religious observances and customs of numerous peoples. Yet the history of religions could not develop as an independent science until two requirements were fulfilled: first, the intellectual climate had to be such that the unbiased study of religious phenomena was permissible. Secondly, there had to be easy access to sources of knowledge pertaining to the non-Christian religions. Broadly speaking, the unimpeded study of the history of religions has only been possible since the age of Enlightenment. The real work could not begin until ingenious scholars like Anquetil Duperron, Champollion and Grotefend had deciphered the scripts of the ancient Persians, Egyptians and Assyrians at the turn of the nineteenth century and thus unlocked the doors to the ancient religious literatures. A factual, strictly scientific knowledge of the religions of the earth was then ensured. In the century and a half that has since passed, the history of religions has pursued its varied task with youthful enthusiasm and has opened up one area after another of its vast field of study.

In the meantime a scientific approach to the study of religion was evolved which, resting on a fixed principle, co-ordinated the various aspects of the study of the phenomenon religion, of which its history is but one. The scientific approach is characterized by its method: it aims at an unbiased and critical compilation of religious data with a view to ascertaining their religious meaning. This implies that attempts are made to understand a religion, even in its strange and less attractive aspects, as it stands, viz. as a testimony to an encounter between people and a super-human reality. The purpose is to attain insight into the belief of the believers. This approach, which does not permit any explanations attributing religion to non-religious factors, as for example to psychological or social forces, is customarily referred to as the phenomenological method, a term that may warrant further elucidation. One of the branches of the study of religion is the phenomenology of religion. This concept has a dual signification. On the one hand it embraces that branch of learning which classifies religious data in order to arrive at an understanding of the structure of a religion and of the meaning of frequently encountered elements such as the sacrifice, prayer and magic. On the other, it relates to the principle of refraining from passing judgement on the truth and value of any religious phenomena. Anyone wishing to make a scientific study of the manifold expressions of religious consciousness cannot afford to make a distinction between true and false religion. Only after a scholar has acquired a profound knowledge and insight and more particularly a keen understanding of that which is essentially religious, can he gradually and cautiously begin to sift his material and thus learn to distinguish between true and false religiosity, between genuine and spurious religion. Yet this progress towards an evaluation does not undermine the phenomenological principle. This principle sets the norm for the study of religion in all its aspects, and first and foremost for the history of religions in particular.[1]

[1] C. J. Bleeker, "The Relation of the History of Religions

Clearly, the history of religions can only be studied fruitfully by those who are willing to listen without prejudice to what believers have to say about their deepest convictions. Yet a good historian must be capable of more. He must be able to make use of the apparatus built up in such fields as the sociology of religion, the psychology of religion, phenomenology and the philosophy of religion. Generally speaking, the historian will not be greatly concerned with the last, although it can teach him to define his terms more closely. But he will have to pay great attention to the sociological and psychological background of the religious date he is examining. Furthermore he should make use of the available phenomenological insights, as these may be of heuristic value to his investigations.

This outline of the principles and apparatus of the history of religions is meant to serve as an introduction to a brief summary of those historical insights that are relevant to our problem. This restriction should be noted. Only a selection of the results and conclusions arrived at by historians of religion will be presented here, namely, those which have a direct bearing on our evaluation of the non-Christian religions.[2] For

to kindred religious sciences", *Numen*, Vol I, Fasc. 2; "The Future Task of the History of Religions", *Numen*, Vol. VII, Fasc. 2, 3.

[2] Although for the sake of brevity we have attributed these results to the study of the history of religion, they are chiefly derived from the study of the phenomenology of religion and what is called comparative religion.

fuller information on this subject the reader is referred to the standard historical and phenomenological works. After these brief observations we shall now turn to the distinctive features of religious life in its manifold forms.

(1) Religion is a universal human phenomenon. Everywhere in the world and at all times since the evolution of *homo sapiens*, people both collectively and individually have worshipped superhuman forces. No tribe or nation has ever been found that was wholly without a religious consciousness. Such a statement is only correct so long as it is realized that in certain cases the religious consciousness finds expression not so much in religious notions as in sacral actions. In the words of R. R. Marett: "savage religion is something not so much thought out as danced out." For the impartial investigator religion, even thus masked, is recognizable because the practised eye readily discerns the fear of the Holy, which is characteristic of true religion. Hence religious belief is inherent in human nature. Nevertheless disbelief has been widespread since the dawn of history. It would therefore be presumptuous to say that every human being is religiously disposed. The psychological question of the origin of disbelief and godlessness, however important it may be in itself, need not be raised here. The remarkable circumstance that religion often arises spontaneously in times and societies that are com-

pletely atheistic is a strong argument in support of the view that religion is a universal human phenomenon. The aforementioned fact that religion occurs in all ages and in one form or another throughout the world may not of course be interpreted as a proof of the existence of God. It is, however, an impressive testimony to the firm hold which religion has always had and still has on the human mind. This means that Christians should not shut their eyes to the undeniable fact that religious belief in whatever guise it may assume is a spiritual power of the first magnitude.

(2) It has over the years become abundantly clear that there is little point in trying to ascertain the origins of religion. The motives for this inquiry were twofold: some scholars hoped to discover in prehistory the basic principle, that is to be able to observe religion in its purest form at the moment of its coming into being; other cherished the expectation that the point would be found where religion was generated from non-religious factors before the very eyes of the observer. In the latter case there was usually a strong desire to derive from this discovery the proof that religion could be fully explained psychologically and anthropologically and was therefore a phenomenon that ought to disappear automatically in enlightened times. The search for the origins of religion has been wont to move in two directions: towards prehistory and towards the study of the religions of non-literate

societies. Explanations for the failure of this search
are not far to seek. Prehistory only gives the vaguest
of answers to the question asked. The tokens of religious consciousness among the earliest earthdwel-
lers in the form of spirit and ancestor worship, the
cult of the sun or the great mother are interesting, but
they are so difficult to interpret that no information on
the dawnings of religious consciousness can be gather-
ed from them. Neither can it reasonably be expected
that the study of religions of non-literate peoples will
yield any insight into the origins of religion. The
primitive religions are not manifestations of the beginnings of human civilization. Before they became
an object of study they had existed for an indefinite
period of time and developed however slowly in some
way or other. Hence it cannot be expected that the
primitive types of religion mark the starting-point of
the history of religions. From an historical point of
view this question is insoluble.

The only meaningful question is that concerning
the ideological intention. This means searching for
the moments when religious belief wells up spontaneously in human hearts. This event still takes place
today and is just as marvellous and inexplicable as
ever. In the course of the centuries living faith has
arisen in a spectacular fashion wherever divine messengers have appeared to preach a new truth or reformers
have set about their missions of purifying and reviving

a forgotten and fundamental idea. In this process the consequences of natural factors such as historical background, climate, race or psychological make-up of the persons concerned have no doubt played a part. Yet the underlying reason for the rise of a new type of religion has not yielded to investigation. Historians of religion are not entitled to introduce the theological conception of revelation here. It may and must, however, be urged that religion evidently arises when a particular truth thrusts itself imperatively upon people who are receptive to it. Whatever is applicable to the religious consciousness within the bounds of history must also be valid for primeval times. This is all that can be said of the historical origins of religions.

Such a conclusion casts new light upon the multiformity of religion. Only to a very limited extent can this be explained from natural factors, such as national character, climate and so forth. In order to understand this we must draw distinctions between various human characteristics. As far as their basic inclinations and reactions are concerned people are alike all the world over, even though it is possible to discern differences of temperament which may conceivably be attributed to nationality. In their way of thinking and their value-judgements, however, people diverge greatly. A comparison, for instance, between the intellectual world of primitive man and that of an academically educated man of the twentieth century will make this clear. The outlooks of various Eastern peoples are by no means uniform and they differ again in certain particulars from Western behaviour patterns. These differences are determined by the cultural heritage shared by the peoples in question. The rise of cultures and their peculiarities are also inexplicable. As H. Nakamura has shown in his extremely interesting study, the differences between the Indian, Chinese and Japanese ways of thinking cannot be traced to climatological, geographical, racial, social or other similar factors.[1] Hence it is not to be wondered at that the diversity of conceptions of religious truth resists reasonable explanation. An objective observer cannot, however, fail to conclude that these differences are not arbitrary. They have arisen apparently spontaneously and as a result of an inner necessity, when certain groups of people have felt themselves compelled—sometimes at the instigation of an originally minded leader—to accept as standard a particular style of religious life. So, although we may not know the reasons for these differences, their existence cannot be denied and therefore may not be ignored in the confrontation of Christianity with the non-Christian religions.[2]

(3) In a confrontation of Christianity with the non-Christian religions we must be clear about which definition of religion we are using. The broader the defi-

---

[1] H. Nakamura, *The Ways of Thinking of Eastern Peoples*, 1960.
[2] C. J. Bleeker, *De structuur van de godsdienst*, pp. 84f.

nition, the larger will be the area of religious history which will have to be evaluated from a Christian viewpoint. The narrowest definition comprises only that which is circumscribed by the Christian faith; this would dispose of our entire problem, and the history of religions would not even enter the picture. Even those who are prepared to draw upon historical knowledge may, however, impose drastic restrictions. Some scholars use belief in a personal God as the criterion of true religion. A definition of this kind inevitably excludes important and essential aspects of the history of religions, as for example a large part of primitive religion, certain forms of mysticism and Buddhism, at least in its original guise. Buddhism is in fact the famous test-case. Although Buddha never wished to commit himself on the question of whether a god or gods existed, it would be absurd to strike his doctrine of salvation from the list of religions.

The formulation of a definition of religion is indeed an interesting but extremely difficult problem. We shall refrain from giving a survey and a critical analysis of all the attempts that have been made.[1] All that concerns us now is the finding of a definition that will give the non-Christian forms of religion their due. To my mind such a definition should be so inclusive as to contain all the phenomena that the trained and

[1] C. J. Bleeker, "The Key-word of Religion", *The Sacred Bridge*, 1963.

impartial investigator recognizes as religious, and at the same time so exclusive as to bar all forms of pseudo-, or as Tillich calls them, quasi-religions. Söderblom provided us with a definition of this kind, when he wrote: "Fromm ist der, für den es etwas Heiliges gibt".[1] Consciousness of the Holy may be present where clear-cut notions of a transcendent reality are lacking; while it is also a guarantee that the concern is not directed towards values that have only a relative and individual significance. Tillich has formulated the essential characteristics of religion as follows:

> Religion is the state of being grasped by an ultimate concern, a concern which qualifies all other concerns as preliminary and which itself contains the answer to the question of the meaning of our life. Therefore this concern is unconditionally serious and shows a willingness to sacrifice any finite concern which is in conflict with it.[2]

This is a succinct definition to which every historian of religion can subscribe, since it is both precise and comprehensive. The profundity, the wealth of ideas, the purity of the diverse forms of religious belief, the deep seriousness and heartfeltness with which believers of every creed profess the truth that is holy to them cannot fail to impress any student of this subject.

[1] N. Söderblom, *Das Werden des Gottesglaubens*, 1916, p. 193.
[2] P. Tillich, *Christianity and the Encounter of the World Religions*, 1963, pp. 4-5.

(4) In studies on the history of religions the various religions are frequently depicted in rather an idealized fashion. Anyone who is more closely acquainted with specific religions, either through source-material in the case of the religions of the past, or by observation of the behaviour of those who profess to the living religions, will not fall into this attitude. Many Christians find the strange features and outward manifestations of certain religions offensive and condemnable. This is a serious problem. Those religious phenomena which are wholly exotic can only be understood if one is prepared to set aside momentarily one's own spiritual beliefs and transport oneself mentally into another realm of religious feeling. As a man can understand his fellow men despite differences in race and background, indeed even despite linguistic barriers, so too a person who knows what religion is can learn to understand a fellow believer, even if the latter adheres to a strange belief.

The study of ancient religions provides striking instances of a further difficulty to be overcome. For these religions display features that modern man and Christians in particular are apt to consider as immoral, namely the forms of sexual symbolism and the sexual rites which are integral to and shamelessly evident in these religions. Conspicuous examples are not hard to find. The notion of the world having been created by coitus or masturbation; the idea of androgynous gods, of the virgin-mother and of the god who, as is recorded in Egyptian mythology, "is the bull of his mother", that is who impregnates his mother; the worship of the male and female genitals; sacral prostitution and ritual nakedness. An orthodox Freudian will perhaps deem these phenomena to be proof of the thesis that religion is concealed libido. Others see in them a radical corruption of religion by immoral passions. Both assumptions are incorrect. Although it cannot be denied that eros plays an important part in religion, there is no question of an "eroticization" of religious life in antiquity. To begin with, it may be recalled that ancient man looked upon these expressions of sexual life as completely natural and spoke of them with no sense of shame or perversity. Indeed, it may be claimed that he saw in sexuality the divine and creative force. And as the cosmos was his only source of knowledge of God and he lacked other images, it is understandable that he often seized upon sexual symbols to express his realization that the deity possessed the power of spontaneous creation. Broadly speaking, this is the meaning of the sexual symbols and rites mentioned above. A detailed analysis of each of these lies outside the scope of this section.

At the same time there is no need to conceal the fact that in certain cases sexuality has indeed considerably contaminated religion. But this oft maligned basic drive is not alone in this respect. Other human passions such as ambition, thirst for power and vanity have frequently been allowed free rein under the guise of piety. Accordingly, no serious students of the history of religions, including that of Christianity, can afford to be blind to the flaws in all religions. These flaws do not consist in irreligious phenomena alone. In every religion ideas and customs may be found which no longer possess religious content and are borne along as dead matter in the stream of living faith. It is useful to draw attention to these facts. For there is a tendency to make a caricature of a strange belief that appears distasteful. When such a grotesque picture of the non-Christian religions is compared with Christianity in its ideal form, the result is inevitably an evaluation which is scientifically inaccurate and morally unjust. Every religion, Christianity not excepted, has its weak spots. Anyone wishing to compare Christianity with the non-Christian religions is certainly entitled to indicate the less desirable qualities in the latter, but first he should do justice to their central idea.

(5) One of the generally accepted results of phenomenological inquiry is the thesis that the formal structure of a religion falls into three parts. In religion there are three recurring factors, namely God, man, and the relation between God and man, which is expressed in the cult and in the observance of God's laws in man's personal and social life. To put it differ-

ently, we may say that a religion is made up of (a) a
holy vision of a Supreme Being or of the being and
will of the Deity, (b) a holy path that a man must
pursue in order to be freed from his sin and suffering
and (c) a holy action that the believer must carry out
in the cult and in his personal religious life. Of these
three factors the notion of God possesses logical
priority; for it is the nature of the holy vision that
determines the character of the holy path and the holy
action and makes them comprehensible. In this complex of ideas the inner logic of the religion is revealed.

It is plain that this phenomenological analysis sepa-
rates elements of the religious phenomena which are
in reality indivisible. It may at times prove difficult to
isolate one of the three constituent parts of a religion.
The notion of God, for example, is not immediately
perceptible in certain forms of primitive religion although it is present by implication. Cases also occur
in which one of the three components is either scarcely
demonstrable or appears in an unusual guise. Buddhism in its original form had no cult in the true sense
of the word (a logical consequence of the doctrine of
Buddha which lacks the notion of God) while certain
types of mysticism cannot strictly speaking be said
to possess cults either. On the other hand the pri-
mordial religious vision of certain religions, for
instance ancient religions and some Eastern ones, finds
almost complete expression in the cult. In order to

understand these religions one must discard the axiom which prevails among Christian theologians and Western intellectuals that the essence of a religion must be comprised in a specific dogma. Briefly stated, the thesis that the structure of a religion falls into three parts is of value inasmuch as it increases our ability to recognize the genuine constituent elements of both Christianity and the non-Christian religions.

(6) In addition to these formal characteristics phenomenologists have also drawn attention to structural relations of a more substantial nature which reveal the logical construction of the religious phenomena. Religions are extremely complex organisms. In the course of its existence every religion has absorbed various heterogeneous elements. Such subsidiary matters should not prevent the phenomenologist from tracing and laying bare the factors underlying the ideological structure of religion. They would appear to be the following:[1]

(a) The number of ways in which religious belief expresses itself is relatively limited. The same religious symbols are found throughout the world. These parallels soon attracted attention and have been the subject of many studies in the field of comparative religion. They are indeed of great interest. The relation between God and man is, for instance, expressed in four constantly recurring images, namely that relation between

[1] C. J. Bleeker, "La structure de la religion", *The Sacred Bridge*.

father and child, master and servant, friend and friend, and lover and beloved. Striking similarities between religions should not, however, blind the student to the fact that the resemblance is usually superficial and that the idea and intention behind identical formulations may be completely different.

(b) Religion is *sui generis* and cannot be explained by non-religious factors. Every religion possesses its own individuality which is irreducible and can only be comprehended and described after long study. It is, however, an illusion to believe that one can ever fathom a religion to which one does not personally profess. It must first and foremost be remembered that the believer keeps a secret which he cannot and does not wish to reveal to non-believers or believers in other faiths. Secondly, while it may be true that the student who is sympathetic towards his subject can acquire the ability to penetrate a considerable distance into another type of belief, he can never make it his own. There is a limit to the extent to which one can identify oneself with something alien to oneself. Nevertheless, it is possible to obtain a view of what is unique in a certain form of religion. Understanding of the difference between the Islamic doctrine of predestination and Calvin's leads, for example, to the discovery of the unique character of Islam. The Calvinist doctrine is founded upon the idea of God's consummate holiness, in the face of which a sinner

cannot continue to exist, so that those who are pre-
served have God's incomprehensible mercy to thank
for their eternal salvation. The Muslim lives under the
crushing weight of the omnipotence of Allah, who
disposes as he pleases. With resignation and courage
the believer accepts the vicissitudes of life confident
that the wise but inscrutable will of Allah has ordained
it thus. Such a remarkable conception of the relation
between God and man, which ultimately remains
puzzling to the outsider and with which he cannot
identify himself is fresh proof of the originality of the
religion.

(c) Every religion has its own distinguishing feature.
This is an element of truth which also occurs in other
religions, though in a subordinate position, but which
especially characterizes one particular religion. When
describing a religion great attention should be paid
to its distinguishing feature. This structural element
may be illustrated by a few examples. The distinguishing feature of the religion of Zarathustra is the notion
of militant piety; Judaism is pervaded by a deep fear
of God's holiness; while Islam is the religion of
boundless surrender and obedience.

(d) The surest method of becoming acquainted
with the structure of a religion is to pose the question:
How do its believers receive their knowledge of God?
It soon becomes evident that there are various types of
"revelation". Or looking at this question from the

viewpoint of the historian of religion, we may say that a higher necessity has obliged various types of believers to adopt different attitudes of belief and to orientate themselves spiritually towards different things. A few examples will illustrate this principle. The ancient religions are founded on a cosmic vision: the universe testifies to a divine order. Indian religious thinking wrestles with the problem of transitoriness and suffering, a problem which is solved when the liberating insight is attained that the finite is but a veil and life itself an illusion. The mystic strives to release himself from all institutionalized forms of worship and to achieve the mortification of the ego in order to behold in complete emptiness and to experience in bliss the fullness of God. Adherents to the historical religions which are based upon prophetic revelation receive their knowledge of God from sacred history, in which divine messengers have appeared as testimony to the way in which God has intervened on behalf of his children throughout the ages. These examples are sufficient clarification of the function and fundamental significance of the believers' attitude.

Insight into the structural elements previously mentioned leads us to conclude that every religion is a meaningful combination of various lines of thought. Without this realization we cannot hope to be fair in our description and evaluation of the non-Christian religions.

(7) Repeated attempts have been made to unravel the tangled skein of the history of religions by classifying the various religions. This is not the place to discuss critically the systems of classification. It goes without saying that the success of such a venture depends upon the validity of the method. Likewise it is clear that every value-judgement jeopardizes objectivity. The historian should remain impartial and avoid any classification involving a scale of values. In the circumstances hopes of arriving at a useful classification would seem rather illusionary. It is, however, possible to make a number of satisfactory divisions, if one is prepared to be guided by the viewpoints dealt with in clause (6) and by the conclusion reached there. Then a number of types of religion may be observed, all differing characteristically from one another. The principal ones are readily distinguished. The religions of non-literate peoples, however much diversity may exist in this field, form one distinct category. Here we encounter a religious apperception which is characterized by a momentary involvement with the Sacred which manifests itself intermittently in nature and the human world. This likewise applies to the religions of antiquity, whose underlying idea has been alluded to in clause (6). Although in point of fact they are beyond our scope here, they deserve mention, not only for their intrinsic value, but also because they are vital to our understanding of the milieu in which

the Biblical kerygma first made itself heard, and because of the influence they exerted upon the religion
of Israel and primitive Christianity. Hinduism and
Buddhism form another type of religion: both point
the way to the liberating realization that this world
and life are but illusion. All mystics speak the same
language wherever they may live: the *visio beatifica*
holds them in thrall. The religion of Zarathustra,
Judaism, Christianity and Islam all belong to the same
typological category, since they may all be traced to
historical revelation. Here this brief survey must
suffice. It is not hard to grasp how the religions
belonging to the types described have assumed their
present form under the influence of the factors mentioned in (6) a, b, c, and d. This series of types could
be sub-divided still further with the aid of the notion
of the distinguishing feature. As such an elaboration
is not our intention here, the reader is referred to the
relevant studies.[1]

B. Assessment of Viewpoints

The problem of the relation of Christianity to the
non-Christian religions is by no means new. Even
primitive Christianity had to define its attitude to
various forms of Hellenistic religiosity, and in particular to the widespread and chameleon-like gnosti-

[1] C. J. Bleeker, *De structuur van de godsdienst*; *The Sacred Bridge*.

cism. Throughout the centuries this question has continually occupied theologians. Yet in another sense the issue is a new one. Never before has Christianity been confronted by the world religions as spiritual forces on such a scale as it is today. Furthermore the world situation demands a new and radical solution to the problem. The peoples of the non-Western world have won their political independence and now claim cultural and social equality with the West. Those who profess to religions other than Christianity will insist with ever increasing urgency on being recognized by Christians as fellow believers.

Since we have entered a new phase in the treatment of this problem, a survey of the ways in which theologians have approached the subject through the ages would be redundant. Competent authors have furnished us with sufficient information in recent studies.[1] Neither is it necessary to attempt an exhaustive analysis of the discussion which is now being held on this subject. It is not the magnitude of this exchange of ideas that is our concern, but a lucid presentation of the various viewpoints. Consequently we shall only quote the opinions of a restricted number of authors who may be deemed representative of certain attitudes.

Before the validity of the various viewpoints can

[1] E. L. Allen and others, *Christianity among the Religions*, 1960; H. de Vos, *Het Christendom en de andere godsdiensten*, 1962.

be assessed, the part the study of the history of religions and the phenomenology of religion can play in the solution of this problem ought to be indicated. In the next section conclusions will be drawn from the historical insights which were developed in clause (6). The question now arises: Can the aforementioned fields of scholarship tell us whether or not an order of significance exists among the religions of the earth? The answer may be brief. As has already been stated the phenomenological method forbids the passing of a verdict upon both the truth and value of religions. After careful inquiry the most one may say is that certain expressions of a religion are authentic or unauthentic and certain believers true or false. Hence these sciences are not capable of constructing a hierarchy of religions. They can nevertheless be of assistance to us in other respects. Firstly, they furnish us with such impressive evidence of non-Christian belief that we cannot but wonder whether it does not contain true knowledge of God. For this reason no theological pronouncement is of value unless it is based upon detailed knowledge of the history of religions and upon considerable understanding of phenomenology. Unfortunately it must be confessed that writings on this subject do not always answer to this requirement. A second way in which these sciences are of use to us is that they lay bare the structure of a religion. The motley world of religious phenomena is found to have a significant structure. The significance of this structure demonstrates the urgency of the issue at hand. For it proves that there is a core of truth which lies beyond man's will in all religions. One factor in this "logic" deserves special attention, namely the occurrence of characteristic types of religion as is described in clause (7) of section A. Taking this typology as a starting-point, it might be argued that the religions in which knowledge of God springs from the domain of the spirit stand on a higher level than the religions that have their roots in nature and the cosmos. It is furthermore conceivable that Christianity would be granted an exceptional position, since its key-note is love, the highest value known to humanity. But in passing such judgements it should be realized that one is overstepping the bounds of that for which the history of religions and the phenomenology of religion can assume responsibility. After this brief summary of the results obtained by study of the history of religions and phenomenology we may now turn to the assessment of the various viewpoints.

(1) *All Religions Are False*

The first viewpoint is that of the "neutral" observer. This may be called "neutral" because those who adopt this viewpoint believe that they as outsiders can be objective in their judgement of the world-religions. There are two versions of this attitude. The first is that of the man who is not interested in religion and who doubts or denies its value. He is of the opinion that all religions are false; they are founded on self-deception, they are the product of psychic and social forces, and hence psychology provides us with a complete explanation for their occurrence. This familiar claim needs little comment. It fails so completely to appreciate the intrinsic character and meaning of religion as these are demonstrated in every study of the history of religions that it carries its own refutation. Anyone who dismisses religion out of hand shows no understanding of the fundamental truth which a great historian has formulated as follows:

> In this mysterious universe, there is one thing of which Man can feel certain. Man himself is certainly not the greatest spiritual presence in the Universe. He understands the Universe only partially, he can control it only slightly, and manifestly he did not bring it into existence. His own presence in the Universe is, for him, an accomplished fact which has not come through any choice or act of his. There is a presence in the Universe that is spiritually greater than Man himself. This presence is not contained either in some of the phenomena or in the sum total of them.[1]

Even those who are not religious themselves should

[1] A. Toynbee, *An Historian's Approach to Religion*, 1956, p. 273.

show sufficient respect for the facts to acknowledge
the existence of true religion.

(2) *All Religions Are Equally True*

Of greater interest is the second version of the
neutral stance, namely that all religions are equally
true. This is the claim of those who can make no religious choice. The motivation behind it is not always
the same. Some of its supporters believe that all historical religons are the imperfect utterances of the same
eternal idea or ideas. Thus in the days of the Enlightenment the thesis was defended that the nucleus of all
religions consisted of three notions: God, virtue and
immortality. Their truth, it was held, was built upon
this ideological foundation. An analogous view may
still be found to exist today, yet only among the
uninformed. For the history of religions clearly
demonstrates that it is quite unthinkable that all religions should share the same fundamental idea. Other
claimants believe in a kind of universal religion which
determines the esoteric nature and the collective truth
of all religions. The reader will recognize this as a
familiar thesis of the theosophists. From it arises the
expectation that all existing forms of religion will
fuse together into this universal belief which will be
the future religion of humanity. These and similar
opinions were voiced at the famous Parliament of Re-

ligions in 1893 and later in the movement for World
Fellowship of Faiths. Thus at the International Congress of this movement in 1935 A. Vail spoke of "the
underlying and eternal unity of the great world religions". F. L. Riley who spent nineteen years on a
comparative study of sixty-one sacred books presented this congress with the description of "one religion in sixty scriptures". Swami Yogananda formulated "what nineteen faiths contribute to spiritual
technique".[1] It goes without saying that such attempts
to grasp the universal essence of the manifold religions
can yield only vague formulations. Furthermore they
proceed from a faulty assumption. Although it is correct to say that all religions have a stake in the truth,
this by no means implies that a sort of common de-
nominator exists which makes them all equally true.
The history of religion clearly indicates that knowledge of God varies in characteristic ways in different
religions. As a believer one must make a choice. A
universal religion is a *fata morgana*. Rudolf Otto once
referred to such a synthetic product as "an Esperanto
religion".

It is significant that the Indian Yogananda took as
his theme at the aforementioned congress "what nineteen faiths contribute to spiritual technique". Behind
this phrase lies concealed the characteristically Indian
conception of the problem of religious truth and of

---

[1] *World Fellowship*, 1935, pp. 581f.; 567f.

the relation between religions. In India only those
truths are appreciated which are found to be effective
in the practice of the religious life in that they help
man to realize his own nature.[1] For religious self-
realization truths from many types of faith may be of
service. For redeeming truth has many aspects and
assumes many forms. Only the man who has acquired
true insight will comprehend this. Whether he shares
in this liberating knowledge depends upon his spiritual maturity. This vision underlies Radhakrishnan's
words:

> The sects of all religions are agreed that there is some-
> thing in the human soul which is related to the abso-
> lute, which is the Absolute. It is the original ground
> of the soul, the meeting point of soul and God, the
> source and basis of all knowledge, all beauty, all good-
> ness, indeed of all ideas of universal significance.[2]

In support of this thesis he quotes from the Upanis-
hads, Buddha, the Old Testament, Mohammed,
Jesus, St. Augustine and Meister Eckhart. It would
be unjust to suspect a thinker like Radhakrishnan of
religious relativism. The passage quoted reveals
rather the characteristically Indian predeliction for
pluriformity of truth and the ability of the Indian to
reconcile with each other religious ideas which are

[1] R. N. Dandekar, "The Characteristics of Eastern Culture",
*Proceedings of the IXth International Congres for the History of Re-
ligions*, 1958, pp. 667f.

[2] Radhakrishnan, *Recovery of Faith*, 1956, p. 148.

to our minds irreconcilable. With all due respect for the value of this vision, this is not a path a Christian can take. His faith is founded on a choice. In actual fact a religious thinker like Radhakrishnan is only seemingly neutral. On closer inspection he interprets religions on the basis of his notions as a Hindu. If one were to incite him to outspokenness he would presumably affirm his belief in the superiority of Hinduism.

In the history of religions and phenomenology of religion judgements or choices are out of place. From a scientific angle this impartiality is completely justified. A neutral position is, however, untenable when the question arises whether all religions are true or false. Both he who maintains that all religions are untrue, and he who claims with a show of quasi- impartiality that they are all equally true, base their claims—frequently unconsciously—on an unexpressed principle. Consequently one cannot condemn the Christian for dealing with the problem from his own point of view, particularly since for the Christian the highest spiritual goods are at stake, namely the nature and extent of God's revelation and the incomparable significance of the gospel. It may, however, be demanded of a Christian who wishes to be worthy of the name of scientific theologian that his opinion is based on an intimate acquaintance with all the material available.

The purpose of this book is to come to a theologically justified conclusion on the relation of Christianity to the non-Christian religions. What will this conclusion be? Broadly speaking, two standpoints are conceivable, namely (1) Only Christianity is true; (2) side by side with the Biblical kerygma which is the final authority for Christians, elements of knowledge of God may be found in the non-Christian religions and as such they call for recognition.

(3) *Only Christianity Is True*

This standpoint is familiar to us all and occurs in two different versions: a rigorous and a more moderate one. So long as Christianity was beleaguered by certain non-Christian beliefs, it adopted the rigorous attitude of branding these other religions as proceeding from Satan or as the result of human wickedness. In more peaceful times when the opportunity arose to become better acquainted with adherents to strange religions, it became more difficult to condemn their piety. The profundity and subtlety of these religions were all too manifest. As a consequence Christians were obliged to alter their views somewhat and to qualify the non-Christian faiths as respectable but tainted expressions of the pious aspirations of men in search of God. This opinion may still be heard today and it always entails the tacit or explicit assumption

that Christianity is the only religion comprising true
knowledge of God acquired by revelation.

(a) Karl Barth's Standpoint

A clear and famous instance of this viewpoint is to
be found in Karl Barth's *Dogmatik* I 2, namely in § 17
which is entitled "Gottes Offenbarung als Aufhebung
der Religion". Here Barth makes many remarks worth
of our consideration on the theological character of
God's revelation and on present-day Christianity as
an institution. The antithesis which he discovers
between "Offenbarung" and "Religion" is, however,
to my mind untenable both theologically and histo-
rically. It is furthermore extremely misleading, since
Barth creates the impression that this solves the problem of the relation between Christianity and the non-
Christian religions. In any case his supporters seem
to assume that in this section of his *Dogmatik* Barth has
had the final say on this subject.[1]

[1] Barth's ideas are discussed at some length mainly on account of the conclusions that have been drawn from this section
of *Dogmatik* I 2. Otherwise this would be virtually unnecessary
in view of the fact that in the first sentences of his great work in
which he defines the basis of his dogmatics, he bars the theological door to the problem that is our prime concern here. These
opening words read: "Dogmatik ist eine theologische Disziplin.
Theologie ist aber eine Funktion der Kirche." The validity of
the leading statement is unquestionable. The subsequent sen-
tence, however, narrows down theology in a manner that is

A selection of quotations will serve to clarify Barth's standpoint. In the section mentioned he writes:

> Religion ist Lebensäusserung des Menschen.[1] Religion ist Unglaube, Religion ist eine Angelegenheit, man muss gerade sagen: die Angelegenheit des gottlosen Menschen. Der Satz formuliert das Urteil der göttlichen Offenbarung über alle Religion. Er ist keine Bestreitung des Wahren, Guten und Schönen, dass wir bei näherem Zusehen in fast allen Religionen entdecken können.[2] Dieses zu-uns-kommen der Wahr-

unacceptable to any theologian with critical leanings and a love of the free and independent quest for the truth. Space does not permit a more profound inquiry into the problem of the essence of theology. Suffice it to say that besides church theology there is an academic, independent theology that allows for certain prolegomena in which issues such as the present one ought to be dealt with, if there are objections to its incorporation under the heading of the doctrine of the revelation. It is characteristic of Barth's viewpoint that he defines the scope of theology thus: "So ist Theologie als biblische Theologie die Frage nach der Begründung, als praktische Theologie die Frage nach dem Ziel, als dogmatische Theologie die Frage nach dem Inhalt der der Kirche eigentümlichen Rede". A subject such as church-history has no independent theological significance in his eyes. The theological function of the history of religions lies beyond his field of vision. Apparently Barth's interest in theology extends no further than the subject to which he is so devoted, namely the establishment of a system of dogma and the elucidation of the Christian faith. The problem that concerns us so greatly here has no fascination for him. He is fully entitled to choose his own subject-matter, but when he reduces theology to a function of the church a strong protest is called for. This view is erroneous and untenable.

[1] p. 324.
[2] p. 327.

heit trifft uns als religiöse Menschen mitten in jenem
Versuch Gott von uns aus zu erkennen... Aber eben
die Religion des Menschen als solche wird durch die
Offenbarung, wird im Glauben an die Offenbarung
aufgedeckt als Widerstand gegen sie. Religion von der
Offenbarung her gesehen wird sichtbar als das Unter-
nehmen des Menschen, dem was Gott in seiner Offenbarung tun will und tut, vorzugreifen, an die Stelle des
göttlichen Werkes ein menschliches Gemächte zu
schieben, will sagen: an die Stelle der göttlichen Wirk-
lichkeit, die sich uns in der Offenbarung darbietet und
darstellt ein Bild von Gott, das der Mensch sich eigen-
sinnig und eigenmächtig entworfen hat.[1] Würde er
(der Mensch) glauben, so würde er hören, in der Religion redet er.[2] Was der Mensch in der Religion will:
Rechtfertigung und Heiligung als sein eigenes Werk.[3]

Nobody would deny Barth the honour of being
the most distinguished dogmatist of our time. His
contribution of a new approach to the formulation of
Christian doctrine has been outstanding. But there
are two respects in which Barth fails completely.
First, he distorts religion; and secondly, he only offers
a pseudo-answer to the question that occupies us here.
So far as the first point is concerned, the picture
Barth paints of religion is a caricature. "Religion als
Unglaube" is nonsensical, a product of the theological
ivory tower. True though it may be that man's re-

[1] p. 329.
[2] p. 330.
[3] p. 338.

ligiosity is interwoven with disbelief, sin, wilfulness and the urge to survive, nevertheless one would be hard pressed to find a religious man who lacks reverence for what is utterly sacred to him. Hence it is untrue to say that in religion man speaks instead of listening with faith. It is untrue that man has wilfully and arbitrarily designed his own image of God. It is untrue that man seeks to justify and sanctify himself by religion. The statement "Religion ist die Angelegenheit des gottlosen Menschen" is an empty phrase. For the truly godless person has no religion. Presumably Barth would counter that I am misconstruing his words since he uses the word religion to mean human unbelief in contrast to belief based on revelation. If so it must be said that his use of words is artificial and arbitrary and apt to give rise to misunderstanding. In current scientific terminology the term "religion" signifies the relationship between man and a transcendent reality. Religion accordingly entails all the rites, practices and ideas that spring from belief in a Supreme Being. It is stating the obvious to claim that religion as it is practised by mankind displays many petty human traits. Such impurities do not in any way undermine the value and truth of religion. All forms of religion are characterized by a belief in "revelation", in other words by the believer's consciousness that he has not invented the redeeming truth but received it. The antithesis between religion and revelation is fictitious. Belief in revelation as opposed to religion is an abstraction, that is to say an artifice which even for the Christian has no basis in reality. The Christian can only understand and believe in God's revelation in Jesus Christ because he reads the Bible with the inspiration of the Holy Spirit. In the Bible the kerygma is indissolubly linked with the religion of Israel and the religious ideas of the early Christians. God's revelation can never be abstracted from "religion". It realizes itself and is invested in human words, gestures and deeds.

The second point of criticism is this. Barth's notions on "Gottesoffenbarung" as "Aufhebung der Religion" becomes questionable if they are to be read —as many contemporary theologians seem to be doing—as the only correct guide to what the Christian attitude should be towards the non-Christian religions. Imagine what would happen if we were to say to a pious non-Christian: Your religion is unbelief. (This is scarcely hypothetical since Barth briefly indicates that his judgement of "Religion" is also applicable to the non-Christian religions.) What would the effect of our qualification be? In the most favourable event the non-Christian in question would not understand the statement at all or would smile distainfully. And otherwise he would show himself to be extremely angry and greatly offended. The fact that a pronouncement on the question in hand must

be such that it can hold its own in the world forum
and be accepted by non-Christians as well, is positive
proof of the unsoundness of Barth's notions. The
natural reaction of a non-Christian demonstrates that
a great advocate of Christian theology has not been
capable of finding a satisfactory solution to a vital
question. For use within the Church § 17 of *Dogmatik*
I 2 may be of spiritual value, but for our purposes no
theological significance can be attached to it. Hence
it may be concluded that the notions we have cited
from Barth do not contribute to the solution of our
problem. It was inevitable that Barth should fail in
this, since nowhere does he actually attempt to bring
the non-Christian religions within the sphere of influence of his dogmatics. He gives the impression
of passing judgement on spiritual factors which he
has not confronted theologically. To acknowledge
that on closer investigation much truth, good and
beauty are to be found in all religions is of little use.
Such an acknowledgement will be of scant interest
to the non-Christian, as will the declaration that
good and devout people are also to be found among
non-Christians. What the non-Christian demands
is recognition of the validity of his knowledge of
God.

Tillich justly remarks that such an exclusive viewpoint is a step backwards in comparison with the
teachings of the New Testament and the Church

Fathers.[1] It is not hard to find in the New Testament pericopes in which Jesus praises the faith of people who do not adhere to Christological notions. The Church Fathers were likewise perfectly capable of distinguishing between the Greek philosophers' ethics and conception of God on the one hand and the utterly reprehensible magic and immoral practices of popular belief on the other. Nobody ever dreamt of casting, say, Plato out into the darkness beyond the knowledge of God, let alone of dooming him to eternal damnation. What was once the case with Plato should now obtain for the believers in the non-Christian religions who as a result of the breathtaking advances in communication of the past fifty years have become our spiritual neighbours. The reason why Barth adopts this unfortunate attitude may be found in his extremely Christocentric doctrine of revelation: to his way of thinking there is no revelation of God without Jesus Christ. This doctrine is only true in the evangelical sense if it is understood as the theological rendition of Christ's appeal to mankind to repent and follow him. But the conclusion Barth draws from this doctrine, namely that apart from in Christ's appeal God has never proclaimed His message to humanity at any other time or place, is completely unevangelical. This viewpoint finds no support in the New Testament. Barth

[1] P. Tillich, *op. cit.*, pp. 32, 34, 35, 44.

furthermore presents his position as a kind of theological Archimedes point, from whence Christians can objectively judge non-Christian religious life without being judged themselves. Such a vantage point does not exist. The image of the impartial judge has long been banned to the realm of wishful thinking in the other sciences. It is high time this happened in theology as well. In determining the relationship between Christianity and the non-Christian religions we cannot restrict ourselves merely to an evaluation of the latter, but must also include Christianity in our appraisal. The confrontation will not be a true one unless it leads us to reflect afresh not only on the essence of Christianity, but also on the principal "motifs" of the gospel and on God's revelation in Jesus Christ. It is too often forgotten that such a confrontation inevitably involves reciprocity of judgement. We shall restrict ourselves to these general remarks here, since this point will be discussed more fully in the next section.

(b) Hendrik Kraemer's Attitude

We now turn to the views held by Dr Hendrik Kraemer, whose opinion, since he is thoroughly familiar with the subject on which he speaks, carries great weight with many persons. Prolonged residence in the East and profound historical scholarship have made him intimately acquainted with various types of non-Christian belief. He has an eye for the vital importance of the encounter between Christianity and the non-Christian religions and is in addition capable of placing this event within the framework of world developments, as is evident from his book *World Cultures and World Religions* (1960). Kraemer has in fact dealt with this issue time and again. Two other books which may be mentioned are his *The Christian Message in a Non-Christian World* (1931), in which the Christian message as understood according to the principle of Biblical realism is contrasted with the non-Christian religions in an endeavour to strengthen the missionary approach of the Church; and *Religion and the Christian Faith* (1956), in which the author studies well-known passages in the Bible which are believed to offer guidance in solving the problem in hand. In a recent book *Why Christianity of All Religions?* (1962) Kraemer has stated his views on this question with great clarity. As this work contains a full yet concise expression of Kraemer's views it is an excellent starting point for a critical examination of his attitude.

Kraemer attributes no absolute value to Christianity. It is one of the many of mankind's religions and as such a mixture of truth and error. Together with all the other religions Christianity must be placed in "the light of the Person of Jesus Christ, who

39/62

is *the* Revelation of God and alone has the authority to criticize every religion" (p. 15). Only "God's Self-revelation in Jesus Christ" is truly absolute (p. 9). In order to find a means of evaluating the degree of truth contained in the non-Christian religions we must return "to the non-derivative, to what is original, to the primary 'given' of Christianity" (p. 72). This original truth is "the revelation of the truth in Jesus Christ as a *given* and *effectual* quantitative reality", a truth upon which the Christian Church is founded. As an historian and authority on Eastern religious life, Kraemer acknowledges "the moral aspects" of the Eastern religions, in his own words "the major and minor evidences of authenticity and nobility, truth and value, whether it be in rites and practices, in institutions, ideas, experiences or people". He even confesses to have been frequently impressed by "the many splendid folk" he met and looked upon as his friends (p. 88). But when he considers the non-Christian religions in the light of "Jesus Christ, in whom the glory full of grace and truth" has been revealed, he is obliged to face up to the fact that "they are all in error". In this light they are all "noble, but misguided and abortive" (p. 93). By this criterion they are found to be "religions of self-redemption, self-justification and self-sanctification" which are "in their ultimate and essential meaning and significance *erroneous*" (p. 94).

Throughout his work Kraemer is frank about his

attitude to the problem in question being governed
by his Christian beliefs; this, in contrast with those
historians of religion who desire to take up a neutral
position from what Kraemer considers to be a mis-
conception on their part of scientific objectivity. What
Kraemer says here so emphatically is in fact a common-
place. In order to evaluate the relation between
Christianity and the non-Christian religions one must
apply some theological standard. A Christian derives
this from the gospel. Such an evaluation should, however, be preceded by an unbiased study of the history
of religions. There are many historians, famous names
among them, who restrict themselves wholly to this
latter field and refuse to commit themselves on
questions of principle. This right cannot be denied
them. This scientific attitude is not only a consequence
of the direction in which their interests lie but it also
proceeds from the phenomenological principle which,
as we have seen, is normative for the study of the
history of religions. The phenomenologist must leave
all value-judgements to the philosopher and theologian. Anyone who expresses a theological opinion on
this matter must be able to justify both his criterion
and the result of his findings. In this respect Kraemer's
theories, despite his assertiveness of tone, are not always perfectly clear or free from weakness.

First, as regards the criterion, it may be observed
that Kraemer gives varying definitions of the nature

of "the non-derivative, the primary 'given' of Christianity". These are "the Person of Jesus Christ" (p. 72), "Jesus Christ Himself and the quality of love revealed in Him" (p. 83), "Jesus Christ and His Kingdom" (p. 117). This fact demonstrates that "the Person of Jesus Christ" which must serve as a criterion of absolute truth remains void of meaning unless more explicit qualifications such as "the quality of love revealed in Him" or "His Kingdom" are added. Yet the moment this is done an element of a "doctrine" derived from the evangelical tradition has been incorporated in the criterion. This is a step Kraemer definitely does not wish to take. Consequently the doubt arises whether it is possible to define "the non-derivative of Christianity", without involving the evangelical tradition. Here a theological problem of great importance is introduced which, to my mind, Kraemer has not been able to solve satisfactorily. This problem may be stated as follows: For a theologian there exist two irrefutable truths: (1) the person of Jesus Christ forms the centre around which the New Testament revolves; (2) the truth of the gospel which is the ultimate authority for all Christians is founded on God's revelation in the person and teachings of Jesus Christ. This latter statement is based upon personal religious convictions. Its significance is that it provides a foundation for the authority of the "gospel". As soon as one begins to use "the gospel" or "the person of Jesus Christ" as a criterion, one has to give the term content. This must inevitably be derived from the New Testament. And hence one becomes involved in all the uncertainties of New Testament studies. Two alternatives then present themselves: either "the non-derivative of Christianity" more precisely defined as "the person of Jesus Christ", remains a formal principle with no practical application, or one gives it content and then it is quite conceivable that on the basis of serious New Testamentary exegesis one arrives at conclusions concerning the person of Jesus Christ which differ from Kraemer's.

The consequences of these alternatives become evident as soon as one critically examines Kraemer's evaluation of the non-Christian religions. In his opinion they are "in their ultimate and essential meaning and significance erroneous". First, it is not clear how this can be deduced from Kraemer's formal criterion of "the person of Jesus Christ". Even if this criterion is given a certain content, the notion of "God's Self-revelation in Jesus Christ" for example, it does not necessarily follow that God has not made himself known to other peoples at other times in ways that have given rise to the non-Christian religions. Why should the revelation in Jesus Christ exclude other forms of self-communication on the part of God? Indeed, it might well be argued that "the quality of God's love as revealed in Jesus Christ" forbids us to assume that He has left the peoples who live and have lived beyond the light spread by the gospel in utter ignorance of Him. Secondly, it is by no means obvious why the non-Christian religions should be characterized as "religions of self-redemption, self-justification and self-sanctification". Such a qualification is in complete contradiction with the testimony offered by believers in these religions and with the results of historical research. Kraemer wishes to impose this mark on the Eastern religions in particular. Admittedly, there are forms of Eastern religion which give the impression of being founded on the principle of self-redemption, but one must tread warily in this matter as appearances are deceptive. In all events it may be stated with certainty that there is no question of a striving for self-redemption and self-justification in the classical religious tradition of India. It is in fact correcter to say that the search for the "Sat", the True, the Enduring which is recognized in a flash of insight as the Foundation of All involves a state of self-oblivion. An illustrious example of this tradition is the figure of Shankara, a profound philosopher and subtle mystic. His mystical doctrine of redemption is not an identification with the Self but a communing with God, as has been convincingly demonstrated by Rudolph Otto. Shankara expressly excludes from his doctrine those forms of mysticism which are permeated with human passions and the urge for self-justification.[1]

Fortunately Kraemer is not always consistent in his evaluation of the non-Christian religions. He also speaks vaguely of "the evidences for revelatory activity on the part of that same God in all religions" (p. 90) and says that "at the very heart of error itself, we are to discover and to recognize that 'God has passed this way'" (p. 103). Once one has gone thus far, one might as well take the step of acknowledging that all religions are founded on legitimate knowledge of God. It is likewise remarkable that Kraemer is not consistent in his claim that "all religions are in error", since he subsequently makes certain reservations in this respect with regard to Islam and Judaism (pp. 107—9). Indeed, it would be absurd to dismiss Judaism as an error and falsehood. Nevertheless, if Kraemer is prepared to attribute a consciousness of religious truth to Judaism, he will also have to acknowledge the fact that the modern Jewish faith lays great weight on 'conversion', in other words it emphasizes man's duty to improve himself morally and spiritually.[2] This notion might seem to come under the heading of "self-justification" which is looked upon as "erroneous" by Kraemer.

[1] R. Otto, *West-östliche Mystik*, 1929.
[2] *Encyclopaedisch Handboek van het Moderne Denken*, 1950, pp. 358 ff.

(c) Conclusion

Summing up, we may say that neither Barth nor Kraemer offers a satisfactory solution to the problem in hand. When all is said and done, Barth fails to open any new theological perspectives. The juxtaposition of "Offenbarung" and "Religion", the latter of which implicitly embraces the non-Christian religions, only serves as an opportunity for him to discourse at length on the nature and content of the Christian faith. To be sure, any Christian who seriously wishes to live by the gospel will always be willing to listen to such a testimony. However, Barth allows the urgent theological problem of whether the non-Christian religions possess any measure of truth, and if so in what respect, to slip through his fingers. Kraemer grapples seriously with the problem but only to come up with a forced solution which is plainly at odds with his sincere appreciation for the non-Christian religions. The title of his book, which he himself is evidently not particularly pleased with, reveals that he too is laying the wrong emphasis. What is at stake is not the question: "Why Christianity of all religions?" For a Christian this is a foregone conclusion because he believes implicitly in the gospel. The real question is: How can we do theological justice to the non-Christian religions? The believers in these religions have a right to be taken seriously. It is not enough to assure them that there is great beauty to be found in their religious beliefs and practices and that they are splendid people. If they are truly religious, a show of sympathy for their devoutness and virtue will leave them unmoved. What they want is recognition of the significance of the knowledge of God to which they profess.

C. THE EVALUATION OF THE NON-CHRISTIAN RELIGIONS

Sufficient attention has been drawn to the immediate importance of the problem in hand. To avoid misunderstanding, however, it is perhaps worth underlining that for the theologian more crucial issues pertaining to the heart of Christian doctrine do exist. Nevertheless, the increasing interpenetration of the various world-religions has bestowed upon this otherwise peripheral problem a hitherto unprecedented urgency. The position and influence of Christianity in the world today is at stake. A religion that withdraws into the ivory tower of its exclusiveness loses its authority and the opportunity to assert itself. Furthermore it must be remembered that this peripheral question has an immediate effect on the central theological issues of the Christian faith, particularly on the question of how the evangelical truth may best be presented in the world today and what its mission should be.

We have already commented on the worthlessness of any evaluation that is not based on historical knowledge and phenomenological insight. It may therefore be desirable to recapitulate the historical insights presented in Section A before pursuing our problem any further. In Section A the conclusion was reached that no scholar of the history of religions and of phenomenology can fail to be impressed by both the pure religious content of numerous expressions of non-Christian religions and the meaningful structure they display.[1] History teaches us that religion is a universal human phenomenon. Its origins cannot be traced: belief would appear to arise spontaneously. From an historical point of view every phenomenon that testifies to an encounter between man and the Holy, in the sense of a transcendent reality, shall be deemed religious. It is clear that every religion has its flaws; yet many practices and notions that appear immoral by modern Christian standards will be seen to be legitimate expressions of a certain type of religion. The formal structure of a religion falls into three parts: the notion of God, the conception of man, and the imperatives governing the fulfilment of sacred acts are the three ever present components. In addition certain constitutive factors may be distinguished in the structure of the various religions: the religious

---

[1] See also: C. J. Bleeker, *Godsdienst, voorheen en thans, beschouwingen over de structuur van het geloof*, pp. 38f.

consciousness has at its disposal a relatively limited number of modes of expression, which means that formal characteristics are sometimes shared by various religions; every religion has its secret and something that is ultimately non-derivative; every religion may be identified by a specific distinguishing feature; every religion rests upon a particular religious apperception, so that knowledge of God is derived from a certain medium, for example, the cosmos or sacred history. The history of religions does not present us with a standard for grading religions along hierarchical lines but it does enable us to classify them according to type.

Such results of historical investigation are undeniably impressive. Consequently it is not surprising that Nathan Söderblom was able to say:

> It is clearly absurd to restrict divine revelation to Christ. Once one has become familiar with extra-Biblical belief in God in China and Japan, India and Persia, Egypt and Babylonia, Greece and Rome, it is quite impossible to remain so exclusive. Either genuine divine revelation is to be found equally *outside* the Bible, or it does not occur *in* the Bible. As matters now stand the history of religions offers us no third alternative.[1]

And on his death-bed Söderblom is reported to have said: "God lives, I can prove it from the history of

[1] J. H. van Veen, *Nathan Söderblom, leven en denken van een godsdiensthistoricus,* 1940, p. 226.

religions." These statements are doubly striking because in Söderblom a profound knowledge of the history of religions was united with a sincere belief in Christ. Nevertheless, Söderblom failed to define the issue sharply enough, or rather he omitted a link in his argument. And that was this: the history of religions can never prove the presence of revelation, which is in itself a typically Christian concept. It can only furnish us with testimonies to a belief in a transcendent reality, testimonies that are so pure and powerful that the Christian theologian is obliged to acknowledge that they are founded on genuine knowledge of God. He then follows in the steps of Paul who said to the Athenians on the Areopagus: "I see that in everything that concerns religion you are uncommonly scrupulous." To my mind, this statement of Paul's opens the only avenue along which we may hope to find a solution to our problem. What we now require is a theological justification of this point of view. Since such an argumentation is bound to be involved, our conclusions concerning the significance of the non-Christian religions may best be presented point by point.

(1) The history of religions teaches us that every religion is the final authority for those who believe in it. W. B. Kristensen has rightly said:

> Believers have always looked upon their religion as an absolute and not a relative factor, as an absolute value.

If we wish to understand them, we must grasp this fact. We must learn to recognize the independent value of each individual religion, for it is only as such that it has existed in the hearts of men. Let us remember that the belief of believers is the sole existing religious reality. If we wish to become familiar with true religion, we shall have to rely exclusively on what believers tell us.[1]

It is the phenomenology of religion in particular that makes us aware of the truth of this. It teaches us to keep an open mind, while at the same time placing us in the position which the French call *engagement*. We are *engagé* because we realize that all religions are a question of the highest value and truth known to man. Being religious is, as it were, a matter of life and death.

(2) The Christian accepts the kerygma of the Bible as an utterly authoritative truth. As has been indicated in the chapter "Christ in Modern Athens", Christ is our contemporary and he makes an appeal to believers which they feel compelled to answer, not from slavish submissiveness, but from inner conviction and in a spirit of freedom and joyfulness.

As soon as one begins to think about this claim, numerous difficult questions arise relating both to the foundations and the content of Christian belief. Here we can only touch upon those points which are most closely connected with our subject. So far as the au-

[1] W. B. Kristensen, *Inleiding tot de godsdienstgeschiedenis*, 1955, p. 22.

thority of the kerygma is concerned, it is clear that this rests on evidence which is completely convincing to a Christian, but which cannot be proved. The Christian is secure in his belief that God's self-disclosure comes to him through the person and preachings of Jesus Christ. This point presents no difficulties. The uncertainties arise when one tries to define the content of the kerygma. The Bible, and the New Testament in particular, informs us of God's revelation. God's words resound in the words of those who testify to this fact. Three fields of scholarship, namely New Testament studies, Biblical theology, and dogmatics are involved in the attempt to separate the Word of God from the words of man. It is not surprising that theologians differ in their opinions of the content of the kerygma and Christology in particular. Since this book does not pretend to be a contribution to the elucidation of this problem, this subject will not be pursued any further. Moreover, an attempt at a definition of the kerygma has already been made in Chapter Two.

Of greater significance to our argument is another consideration which places the nature of Christian belief in its true light. Christians should learn to realize that nothing is to be gained by discussing the Christian faith *in abstracto*. The existential quality of Christianity cannot be ignored. Sartre has defined this concept of existentialism as follows:

...l'homme n'est rien d'autre que ce qu'il se fait. Tel est le premier principe de l'existentialisme... l'homme n'est rien d'autre que son projet, il n'existe que dans la mesure où il se realise... Or, en réalité, pour l'existentialiste, il n'y a pas d'amour que celui qui se construit... il n'y a pas de génie autre que celui qui s'exprime dans des œuvres d'art.[1]

What Sartre says of man, love and creativity also applies to Christianity. A Christian does not doubt the metaphysical truth of the gospel. But he should also be conscious of the fact that the truth behind the Christian faith can only be verified when it becomes reality, in other words, when men under Christ's influence become spiritual beings instead of the creatures of impulse they are by nature. In this sense there is no Christian faith other than that which is expressed in good deeds and brotherly love. At all events it should be borne in mind that in the harsh and pitiless mental climate of today nobody is going to be impressed by Christianity's claims to a unique position among the religions unless it actually demonstrates that it is different. This leads us to the realization that the gospel preaches a perilous truth, that is to say a truth with which we must dare to venture out into a puzzling and chaotic world. This element of risk is an incentive for us to try seriously to come to terms with the claims to truth made by other religions.

[1] Jean Paul Satre, *L'existentialisme est un humanisme*, 1960, pp 22, 55, 56-7.

(3) Anybody who makes a study of the history of religions will discover much to his surprise that the so-called "strange" religions gradually lose their strangeness. This does not mean that the student will ever succeed in fully fathoming a type of religion that is not his own. No religion allows its secret to be wrested from it. Neither is anyone capable of becoming truly familiar with a religion to which he cannot profess with his whole heart. Yet it is possible for the investigator to set aside for a time his own spiritual preconceptions and penetrate into the beliefs of the adherents to another religion. Then one realizes that it is possible to understand the fundamental ideas behind the non-Christian religions, not only on an intellectual but also on an emotional and existential level. Every religion gives its own answer to the universal human question of the meaning of life. To mention a few examples: the ancient religions proclaimed that true wisdom consists of living in accordance with the cosmic order in which the creative and divine power manifests itself. Upon this harmony depend both man's virtue and his happiness. Greek tragedy depicts in a moving fashion how an innocent man can be fated to become guilty. In his tragid downfall he is purified. Brahmanism offers a liberating insight into the tormenting riddle of the instability and deceptiveness of life. The seeker who succeeds in identifying his own self with the Great Self awakens

from the nightmare of existence. Jainism teaches that man can only become free by means of the most rigorous asceticism: if man really wishes to be himself he must repudiate all earthly goods. Buddhism offers a radical solution to one of the worst torments of earthly existence, namely, suffering. Only by recognizing that the passions are the cause of suffering and by consciously deciding to eliminate them can man escape the cycle of births and rebirths and enter Nirvana where the flame of passion and consciousness is extinguished. Islam emphasizes God's awe inspiring omnipotence and exhorts man to accept the vicissitudes of life as emanating from the inscrutable will of God.

The Christian can understand these beliefs concerning the meaning of life, even though he is not able to accept them fully as his own. A man's spiritual life and conception of truth is far more complicated than is generally realized. It is an illusion to believe that a person lives by one principle and one alone, the truth of the gospel for example. In reality he constantly fluctuates between various moods and outlooks, because life is so complicated that it continually evokes a different human reaction and unlocks the door to changing dimensions of truth. The Christian can therefore learn to grasp the fundamental notions behind the aforementioned religions as diverse religious conceptions of man's existence. Once he has done this he will also acknowledge their share in the truth.

After all, the validity of the claim of the ancients that man can only fare well if he obeys the natural laws cannot be denied. Greek tragedy still fascinates modern man because, despite his will to the contrary, life sometimes involves him in a tragic conflict. Classical Hinduism's conception of life as a cruel illusion is not wholly strange to us. The Brahmin notion of the unassailability of the soul in the midst of illusion and transitoriness is very profound. Jainism has laid bare the roots of man's enslavement: spiritual freedom can only be achieved by the renunciation of all earthly goods. When the Buddhist declares that it is the vanity of man's passions that brings him suffering we cannot but assent. Similarly, we share the Muslim's awe of the sovereignty of God who shapes our destiny.

These religious views all possess human validity, since human existence involves a wide range of experience and offers us a variety of choices in our attitude towards life. They are also true from a spiritual standpoint, since they present themselves not as discoveries made by man, but as a necessity imposed upon him by a divine power. There should be no misunderstanding about this. Owing to the current belief that man's intellectual and technical achievements will soon enable him to control the universe, many persons imagine that they can make of life what they will. Accordingly, they are deluded into thinking that they can explain religion from an exclusively anthropological perspective. But man does not create his religion; it springs from a higher necessity. A striking instance of this has been observed by M. Leenhardt among the Melanesians, whom he describes as having a cosmomorphic rather than anthropomorphic worldview: instead of projecting themselves in the world around them, they recognize themselves to be part of the cosmos.[1] What is true of the Melanisians, is true of all believers. They know themselves to be in the hands of a supernatural force, a divine providence, or truth. They see life and themselves in this light. They are placed in a certain religious position and adopt a system of beliefs which is, as it were, archetypal.

Once this is fully realized, the difficulties arising from the different conceptions of God disappear. The chief stumbling-block would appear to be the distinction between a personal and an impersonal conception of the deity. This difference is not unreal, but it ceases to trouble us if we consider all statements concerning God to be symbolical. The religious symbol is never chosen arbitrarily.[2] It expresses with the greatest possible accuracy in human language what is known of God through revelation. Yet the symbol is

[1] M. Leenhardt, *Do Kamo, la personne et le mythe dans le monde mélanésien*, 1947.

[2] W. B. Kristensen, *Symbool en werkelijkheid*, 1961, 2nd ed.

never wholly adequate. God is neither personal nor impersonal, but supra-personal. The encounter with the Holy may be experienced in different ways: as the hearing of a word and the beholding of a truth. This dissimilarity in religious apperception is reflected in two types of religion and two conceptions of God, namely the personal and the impersonal, the most striking examples of which are Christianity on the one hand, and Hinduism on the other. These two conceptions of God are utterly different from one another, but as forms of knowledge of God they are of equal value.

(4) This train of thought leads us inescapably to the question of how true knowledge of God may be acknowledged apart from in the revelation in Jesus Christ. Down the years various attempts have been made to find a theological basis for knowledge of God outside the framework of the Biblical kerygma. Use has been made of three widely known terms: *logos spermatikos*, universal revelation, and natural theology. None of these terms has ever been really satisfactorily circumscribed. They usually serve to provide a theological *locus* for the knowledge of God that man derives from nature, history and his own life. Attempts to incorporate the non-Christian religions under this heading in a manner that would do them justice have not met with success. Furthermore, no agreement has been reached as to the meaning of these terms. In-

deed, so much uncertainty exists concering their exact definition that it is better to avoid them. The New Testament does not provide an answer to our question either. As was indicated in our second chapter, neither the Gospels, nor Paul's epistles contain any indication how this theological problem might be solved. H. de Vos, in his lucid historical and critical survey of the diverse standpoints has admitted the difficulty quite openly.[1] Being unable to find any support in individual texts, he took "a bold leap" and "chose as his point of departure the Biblical kerygma in its entirety", that is to say the basic motifs of the evangelical proclamation. This theological decision concurs with the approach to this issue that is advocated in this book.

De Vos's words bring us back once more to Paul's sermon on the Areopagus and to Acts 17.22 in particular. When Paul said to the Athenians: "Men of Athens, I see that in everything that concerns religion you are uncommonly scrupulous" and thus acknowledged the value of their form of religion, he was undoubtedly prompted by his deep-rooted confidence in the basic truth of the gospel, namely the proclamation of God's love. Paul has shown us the direction in which we must seek the solution to the problem in question. If we take the Christian belief in the love of God seriously, we cannot possibly assume that God

[1] H. de Vos, *op. cit.*, *loc. cit.*

would allow the peoples who have not had or still do not have the privilege of living in the light of the gospel to wander for centuries in spiritual darkness with only pious, but powerless aspirations for comfort. This vision of God's plan for salvation conflicts flagrantly with His love as Christians know it from the New Testament.

It seems to me that the range of God's love is often unwarrantedly restricted. Christians are inclined to think too exclusively from the point of view of their own need to come to terms with their sense of guilt and sin. God's love is then simply reduced to a quality of forgiveness and mercy which vindicates the sinner. But the love of God should also be thought of as permeating all His transactions with humanity, that is to say His entire revelatory purpose. Such a conclusion leads to one of the first questions which theology in the strict sense of the word, namely as the doctrine concerning God, must deal with, viz. the question of how God has made and makes himself known in the past and present.[1]

---

[1] Here our argument touches on general theological principles which cannot be treated exhaustively. A brief note must suffice. In connection with the remarks made in note 1 on pg. 91/2 it may be contended that the construction of a theological system ought to be preceded by prolegomena in which *inter alia* a provisional evaluation of the results obtained from the study of the history and phenomenology of religions is made. The dogma concerning God should of course form the basis of a theological system. Under this heading it is logical that the

To my mind, the doctrine of revelation should have both an historical and a cosmic dimension. With the recent rapid advances in man's understanding of the universe, his knowledge of the history of mankind, and the ever closer bonds being forged between believers throughout the world, the conception of the revelation must needs be a bold one, one that will embrace both history and the cosmos. In the present context what interests us most is the broad historical perspective which evidence of non-Christian faith has opened to us. God's revelation, however, does not merely extend throughout the world, but it also directs itself personally to individuals.

It is an undeniable fact that apart from the revelation in Jesus Christ God has also made himself known directly to religious people of various types. Evidence of this is to be found in biographies of both celebrated

initial concern should be the question of how knowledge of God is received, and concomitantly the doctrine of revelation. Next should come an inquiry into the Christian conception of the creation and God's providence. Such questions cannot be solved by Christology alone, as some theologians claim. There are problems pertaining to God's role in the life of the individual and in the world, particularly in connection with human suffering and cruelty in nature and human society that cannot be unravelled simply by pointing to God's revelation in Jesus Christ. These are the rocks on which all attempts to base theology on Christology alone must inevitably founder. Neither will attempts to make the doctrine of revelation congruent with Christology ever meet with success. The range of the revelation exceeds that of Christology in every direction.

and unknown believers.[1] The Christian is familiar with this encounter with God from his own experience. To be sure, he acquires the content of his belief chiefly from the gospel. He confesses to a belief bearing a Christian signature because he is borne along by the stream of Christian tradition and because he has consciously chosen his place it in. But it is to God that he owes the fact that he truly believes, that the gospel is a living truth for him; to God who has opened his heart and made Himself known to him in the joys and sorrows of his life and little by little revealed to him the profundity of the truth of the gospel. It is for this reason that Christian doctrine speaks of God's continuing revelation and of the workings of the Holy Spirit which inspires faith and regenerates man.

As a result of these signs of God's immediate concern for man's salvation, we are justified or even obliged to believe that God has lighted the path to truth for all peoples in all ages. The non-Christian religions owe their existence to this fact. The inscrutability of God's wisdom does not permit us to comprehend the purpose that lies behind what we consider to be the essentially different kinds of knowledge of God found in the world-religions. At most we can speak of a pluriformal dispensation of the truth which must be meaningful because comparative studies de-

[1] W. James, *Varieties of Religious Experience*, 1919.

monstrate that the various types of religions have close ideological ties with one another. Indeed, we may say that the religions of the world represent spiritual conceptions of human existence that are complementary to each other. A few examples will demonstrate the validity of this thesis. Thus a re- markable polarity exists between the ancient religions and religions like Brahmanism and Manicheism. The former religions were based on a cosmic vision, characterized by an unshaken faith in the divine order of things, upon which the life of the individual and the community was founded. Brahmanism and Mani- cheism share a pessimistic view of earthly existence and preach, each in its own way, renunciation of the world. Similarly, Buddhism and Christianity com- plement each other to a certain extent, because they represent differing views concerning the exigencies of the human condition: Buddhism offers a solution to the problem of suffering; Christianity clears the way to the conquest of sin. Suffering and sin are the two great enemies of human happiness.

Recognition of the non-Christian religions' claim to a share in man's knowledge of God in no way de- tracts from the exceptional significance of the gospel for Christians. The meaning, however, of the ex- pression "perilous truth" should by now be some- what clearer. In Christ God reveals His love and makes an appeal to man. To avoid misunderstanding it may be said once more that the word of Christ is the final authority for Christians. Yet this word too has its bounds. It should be clearly realized that God has revealed His love in Christ but not His purpose for the world. The gospel exhorts us to *pistis*, to pure and unquestioning trust. It does not offer us gnosis, or knowledge of God's mysteries. As Isaiah so fittingly said, God's ways and thoughts are as far removed from those of man as the heavens are from the earth (Isaiah 55.9). It is upon this plane that we must believe that God's intervention extends beyond Christianity. So although the Christian, who has been granted the truth of the gospel to light his way through life, is part of God's scheme of revelation, whose wisdom he unquestioningly accepts, the truth of the gospel is only true in this hard world in which we live in so far as it is existential, that is to say in so far as it is demonstrated in people's lives. Consequently it is in two respects a perilous truth. This sense of hazard is a noteworthy element in Biblical thinking. Was not the religion of Israel founded chiefly on the overwhelming experience of having been freed from slavery in Egypt rather than on a belief in Jahveh's omnipotence and creative powers? Because Jahveh had delivered the Israelites and made a covenant with them, He was the only God they might serve. This was a perilous belief. Accordingly, the Israelites at first still reckoned with the possible existence of other gods. Later when they

ventured to declare that the God of deliverance was
also the God of the earth and the creator of the universe, the sense of the perilous nature of this belief
remained: suffering and sin continued to give rise
to doubts concerning God's wisdom and goodness,
as is witnessed in the Book of Job and in certain
Psalms (10, 22, 73). God is good, for we know His
love, God is majestic and great and we do not understand Him. We must stake our all on the gospel.

The idea of faith as a perilous truth would appear to
correspond with contemporary man's mode of thinking and conception of life. The world we live in and
the lives we lead have grown so chaotic and incomprehensible that man no longer has an integrated world-
view, embracing all the areas of life in which he moves.
Neither do science and modern philosophy pretend to
have a firm grasp on reality. They explore and try
tentatively to penetrate the darkness of the unknown.
Therefore, a theology which is apprehensive of the
gospel being engulfed by ideas of a universal nature
or by a philosophical *Weltanschauung*, and thereby
losing its specific identity, is not abreast with the times.
Such universal concepts no longer exist. All that can
be said is that the inquiring and thoughtful scholar
perceives bounds within which certain rules apply.[1]
Thus each theory, each conviction only possesses

[1] H. V. van der Hulst and C. A. van Peursen, *Phenomenologie
en Natuurwetenschap*, 1953.

contingent significance. This is true for the Christian faith in particular, as modern man fully realizes. When all is said and done, nobody can prove the existence of God even though we are assured that He rules the universe. The terrible suffering with which man is afflicted remains a vexing problem to everyone that trusts in God's love. Considering the wickedness and injustice rife in the world there is no guarantee that the love preached by Christ will always prevail. Nevertheless, the Christian who is unshakable in his faith clings to the truth of the gospel.

This view of the significance of the Christian faith clearly affects both the position of Christianity today and the relationship between Christianity and the non-Christian religions as it should be. These questions will be dealt with in the next chapter.

THE FUTURE OF RELIGION

It is only right that this study should conclude with a brief examination of the future of religion, for there would be no point in discussing the attitude Christianity should adopt towards modern culture on the one hand and the non-Christian religions on the other, if religion as such were doomed to die. An inquiry into the *status quo* and an attempt to come to terms with the problems involved would then be a waste of time. This book has in fact been based on the implicit assumption that there is still a future for religion. Such an assumption ought, however, to be verified, and in order to do this the three following points must be dealt with: (1) the future of religion as such; (2) the future prospects of Christianity; (3) the future attitude of Christianity towards the non-Christian religions.

Religion

A believer cannot imagine that religion will ever vanish from the earth. Yet it is not unreasonable to ask whether religion too is not subject to the law of transiency, which applies to all earthly things. After all, viewed objectively, religion is a cultural phenomenon, and history teaches us that through the centuries many cultural assets, some of them of the highest quality, have been lost and that many religions have passed away. We have only to recall the ancient religions, the mysteries of the Hellenistic era, or Manicheism, the belief whose adherents were scattered almost from the Pacific Ocean to the Atlantic for a thousand years, to realize that although these religions provided tens of thousands of people with spiritual nourishment, they have now vanished for ever. Theoretically, it is not inconceivable that religion in general should suffer the same fate. In Buddhism of a later date this is considered a very real possibility and hence the eventual disappearance of the teachings of Buddha are anticipated. In this process four periods are distinguished: (1) the first half millennium after the death of Buddha, which forms the golden age of Buddhism; (2) a thousand years of iconolatry; (3) the period of the "last days of the law" (of Buddha), likewise of a thousand years; and (4) the period of the "destruction of the law".[1] This view is clearly derived from the familiar Indian notion of dividing world history into four periods which reveal a downward trend. This, however, does not detract from the significance of this view of human history, entailing the complete disappearance of religion.

In the West many persons share the same con-

[1] Chantepie, *Lehrbuch der Religionsgeschichte* I, pp. 385-6.

viction, although for other reasons and with different motives. Here too the wish is usually the father of the thought. The claim that religion's days are numbered often springs from indifference or hatred of all forms of belief. The history of atheism and materialism is a long one.[1] Disbelief and hostility to belief in a transcendental power have gone hand in hand with religion since early antiquity. This is not to be wondered at, for religious people have committed so many crimes under the cover of piety that doubts as to the authenticity and truth of religion seem highly justifiable. We need not dwell upon this sad story here, but it may be pointed out that we would do well to trace the diverse motives behind various forms of atheism. Paradoxical though it may sound, atheism can conceal a religious pathos in that it may be a defence against certain institutionalized religious notions and customs unworthy of true religion. Thus Xenophanes' grim mockery of the all too anthropomorphic Greek gods sprang from his conviction that there could be only One, the ἀρχή, who could be divine, and not many.[2] Equally interesting is Indian "atheism", which found its classical form in Buddhism. This was not intended as a denial of the existence of a transcendent reality, but as a means of combatting polytheism and all the super-

[1] F. A. Lange, *Geschichte des Materialismus*, 1905.
[2] R. Pettazzoni, *La religion dans la Grece antique*, 1953. pp. 136-7.

stitious and immoral practices attached to it in India.[1]

Accordingly, we must always be prepared to inquire into the motives behind the assurance that religion has outlived itself. In this connection particular attention should be paid to the following three *Weltanschauungen*. First, the widespread and mercurial nihilism in contemporary society.[2] Briefly, this is an attitude of mind that refuses to accept the authority of any established values. Its character and the question whether such a denial of norms can be sustained may be argued at length. As a protest against a false veneration of pseudo-values nihilism is understandable and will remain a factor to be reckoned with. It seems unlikely, however, that the average man will ever be able to live for long without moral and spiritual support. Nevertheless, it is a fact that nihilism fosters an unhealthy climate for the survival and growth of religion. The second world-view that threatens the future of religion is of a different and nobler calibre. This is modern humanism which adopts the attitude that the only imperative is the recognition of man's own worth. Humanism is likewise a complex phenomenon comprising diverse trends. Thus we may encounter humanists who display a lesser or greater degree of religious feeling. Understandably, we are only concerned here with that branch of humanism

[1] H. von Glasenapp, *Der Hinduismus*, 1922, pp. 154 ff.
[2] P. Smits, *Op zoek naar nihilisme* (Oration), 1959.

which denies the existence of a metaphysical reality and which is generally indifferent rather than hostile to religion. It has acquired a certain reputation because an increasing number of intellectuals find themselves drawn towards its principles. Clearly, humanists of this kind will not believe in the viability of religion, even though they do not openly proclaim an impending decease. Far more forcible than the arguments that the nihilists and humanists can and wish to present are thirdly those brought forward by thinkers who consider themselves capable of predicting the disappearance of religion on the basis of their interpretation of history. This point of view may be illustrated by several striking examples. As we are dealing with wellknown theories, a brief characterization will suffice.

Comte's law of the three stages in all human development, the theological, the metaphysical and the positive, is familiar.[1] It will be recalled that, according to Comte, humanity gradually rose in the first stage from fetichism by way of polytheism to monotheism. In the metaphysical period reality was explained by principles and abstractions. In the positive stage, to which humanity has finally progressed only factual knowledge is of any account, and laws embracing general or particular facts are established by means of observation. As a result of the development of human

[1] A. Comte, *Cours de philosophie positive*, 1877.

thought modern man has outgrown religion. Comte's philosophy has been revived in our day in a neo-positivism which holds many minds, consciously or unconsciously, in its sway. Thus it is not surprising that the opinion is often voiced that there can be no future for religion because it is based on an outmoded way of thinking.

This line of argument is likewise followed by all convinced Marxists, although their reasoning is very different. According to Marxist doctrine culture and religion are an epiphenomenon of the production process. In capitalist societies ambitious princes and wily priests make use of religion in order to keep the masses under control. Religion is nothing but "priestly fraud" and "opium for the masses". As soon as society abandons the capitalist system in accordance with the laws of dialectic materialism, religion will be at an end. The Marxist has an incontrovertible belief in the classless Utopia and therefore views godlessness as a liberation from harmful prejudices. In the Soviet Union, the ideological offspring of the theories of Marx, Engels and Lenin, we know that the war against religion fluctuates in intensity. According to the most recent information, this campaign, conducted in scholarly and popular antireligious publications, displays and exhibitions, has not achieved the desired result. Religion has survived and what is more it has been purified.[1]

Phenomenologically the attitude of the godless is most interesting. They passionately profess to a faith without God. It is likewise remarkable that the social-ist-communist movement has from its beginnings made use of slogans and symbols displaying a striking structural similarity to common religious forms of expression, with this difference, however, that they are entirely secular.[2] Evidently, even the man that denies the existence of God cannot avoid thinking along religious lines. This fact is certainly not without significance for the future of religion. Both positivism and Marxism base their claim that religion will disappear on the theory that the progress in man's way of thinking and the development of society will make religion redundant. The ensuing war on religion is usually conducted along rationalistic lines. Attempts are made to demonstrate the illogicality of belief in God.

Quite a different approach has been chosen by the Dutch writer Simon Vestdijk in his sensational book *De toekomst der religie*, published in 1947. Vestdijk wishes to explain religion psychologically. He realizes that psychological insight can be more damaging than all the rational objections to religion. Psychology reveals religion to be a product of projection in the

[1] Constantin de Grunwald, "Science et Religion en Union Soviétique", *Archives de Sociologie des Religions*, 16, July-December, 1963.

[2] H. de Man, *Zur Psychologie des Sozialismus*, 1927.

sense defined by Feuerbach in his *Das Wesen des Christentums*, that is to say that religion should be seen as answering to certain anthropological needs. As a result of a sense of his own impotence and imperfection man projects on the screen of nothingness the image of an omnipotent and perfect God whom he worships and from whom he expects salvation. On the basis of this thesis Vestdijk presents an ingenious new theory concerning future prospects. He distinguishes between three religious types, namely, the metaphysical, the social and the mystical. The first type, of which he takes Calvinism to be the classic example, is a complete projection. Social man sees his ideals embodied in his fellow men, and the mystic strives to realize the ideal in his own life by means of introspection. In Vestdijk's opinion the metaphysical type is doomed to disappear. This means that Christianity's days are numbered. Vestdijk pretends to regret this fact and hopes that the liquidation of Christianity will be carried out in a manner worthy of it. Partly as a consequence of the flow of ideas from the East a socio-mystical religiosity of the Buddhistic type will, in his opinion, gradually gain the upper hand and differences in belief will become so subtle that, as Vestdijk writes: "true Christians, awakening in the morning after a good night's sleep will be capable of wondering: 'Am I not really a Buddhist?'" In future man will be trained in psychoanalysis, and a new type of *homo religiosus* will arise with a candid approach to sexuality and satisfactorily adjusted to the inevitability of death and to feelings of resentment.

Such a vision of the future of religion cannot be refuted by theological arguments, based as they are on the believer's personal convictions which bear no weight with the non-believer. The history of religions and phenomenology provide us with a better weapon against this attack. They present *sine ira ac studio* a number of arguments, from which the conclusion may be drawn that religion by no means lacks a future. First, we may recall the results of historical and phenomenological investigations, as these have been described in Chapter Three. They demonstrate that religious feeling is fundamental to human nature, so that it may scarcely be assumed that religion will vanish without trace. Secondly, religion has been found to possess a logical structure. The "logic" that is unfolded in religious phenomena justifies the view that religion does not merely spring from natural human urges, but is born of a higher necessity. Furthermore, the afore-named sciences also cast light on the knotty problems connected with the progress of religion.[1] To answer the question whether religion still has a future it is essential to know something of its development throughout the history of mankind. The

[1] C. J. Bleeker, "Some Remarks on the 'Entelecheia' of Religious Phenomena", *The Sacred Bridge*.

past always contains some signs pointing to what may be expected to happen in the future. However, it is generally accepted that the nature and meaning of historical development is one of the most difficult philosophical problems.[1] The various schools of thought are therefore widely divergent. In the nineteenth century the conviction reigned that history reflected man's progress to enlightenment and freedom and that, by virtue of the spectacular developments in science and technology, humanity would soon enter the kingdom of eternal peace. The twentieth century, on the other hand, has brought countless variations on the theme of Otto Spengler's prophesy of "the decline of the West". The rate of growth is on the decline: Western culture is fading. Even more precarious than the endeavour to determine the course of world-history is the attempt to trace any clear line of development in religion. Nevertheless, the task is not entirely hopeless. Proof of this are the notes made by Rudolf Otto on "Parallelen und Konvergenzen in der Religionsgeschichte".[2] If we further explore the possibilities opened by him we come to realize that a certain dynamic force is at work in the world of religious phenomena. As the framework of this

[1] C. J. Bleeker, "Het begrip 'ontwikkeling' in de godsdienstgeschiedenis", *Vox Theologica*, Oct., 1930.

[2] R. Otto, *Das Gefühl des Überweltlichen, sensus numinis*, 1952, pp. 282f.

book precludes a thorough examination of this question, a few indications must suffice.

It is remarkable that the leap forward from the primitive to the ancient stage of religion came about almost simultaneously in the fourth millennium B.C. in both of the oldest centres of civilization in the Middle East, Egypt and Mesopotamia. Likewise it may be observed that parallel religious events took place in Israel, Greece, India and China in two different periods before Christ. In Israel the first prophets appeared in the eigth and seventh centuries. In Greece a higher type of religion came into being. In India Brahmanism evolved while China entered the historic epoch of the awakening of religious thinking. This was, as it were, the crest of the first wave. A second followed between the sixth and fourth centuries. It was during this period that Ezekiel and the so-called second Isaiah preached a universal monotheism, that Plato and Aristoteles propounded their far-reaching ideas, that Lao-tse and Confucius spread their philosophies and Buddha proclaimed his doctrine of salvation. The beginning of our era was also a period of tremendous activity, not only on account of the birth of Jesus Christ but also because spectacular changes were taking place in the religious life of the East. Brahmanism, which had gone into a decline with the rise of Buddhism, went through a revival, while in Buddhism itself the Mahayana system evolved, which formed the impetus that raised Buddhism into a world-religion. All these phenomena are slight but unmistakable symptoms of the rhythmical way in which the history of religions moves forward. With the ever increasing disintegration of religious life in more modern times it has become virtually impossible to chart the ebb and flow in this period. During the last few hundred years the world-religions have been moving towards a state of crisis. On the one hand their chances of survival are in the balance, yet on the other they have been undergoing a process of purification. From time to time an event takes place in all these religions that deserves our attention here. This is the periodic occurence of a religious revival, reminiscent of a slow-motion chain reaction. That is to say, believers suddenly come forth who give an entirely fresh interpretation to the fundamental truth of their religion and thus unleash latent forces in the traditional beliefs. Thus time and again a religion cleanses itself from within and ascends to a higher spiritual level. Out of the recurrent tragic decline in spiritual standards is born anew a passionate desire for restored and renewed belief. This circumstance proves that religion possesses an indestructible source of power on which it can draw to replenish itself, and that the religious principle never wholly deserts mankind. At the same time this source of power guarantees a future for religion.

On the strength of such a conclusion we may perhaps venture to present a few ideas relating to the task that lies before religion in the years ahead. Clearly, it would be a risky enterprise to prescribe a line of conduct possessing world-wide validity. The difference between religious attitudes in, say, the East and the West is one of day and night. J. Herbert has characterized life in the East thus: "Les préoccupations métaphysiques, religieuses, spirituelles et mystiques, avec tout le ritualisme qui les accompagne, sont le principal fondement de la vie asienne traditionelle; elles en imprègnent tous les domaines, de la vie familiale et sociale à la science et à l'art".[1] In the West culture has been greatly secularized and religion has been forced to be on the defensive. One thing, however, is certain, we in the West may in truth say to our fellow men in the East: *hodie mihi, cras tibi*, for in time religion throughout the world and consequently in the East too will be cast into the melting-pot. Modern culture is quickly spreading to the four corners of the earth and it will not fail to undermine age-old traditions. The religious crisis will impinge on all forms of belief. Nevertheless, there are signs that a purer form of religion may arise from this threatening and hostile age. Whatever the outcome of this struggle for existence may be, one truth is irrefutable: the maxim *sit ut est aut non sit* applies equally to re-

[1] J. Herbert, *Introduction à l'Asie*, 1960, p. 39.

ligion. A religion that surrenders its original character is devoid of significance. Theologians must resist the temptation to conform for popularity's sake to humanism or any other philosophical system which may gain ground in the future. Religion is service to God not service to man, although an immediate consequence of true religion is the desire to promote the well-being of one's fellow men. There is, however, nothing to be gained by religion's conforming to the ways of the world. Only those types of religion that preach a truth utterly different from the wisdom of this world have a right to survive. Difficult though it may be to say exactly what the content of this truth should be, because the basic religious conceptions of the great world-religions differ so widely, we may nevertheless be sure that it involves man's relation to the transcendent reality we are wont to call God, the believer's moral code and way of life and his eternal salvation. These matters pertaining as they do to the highest and most enduring values are not to be trifled with. Hence every religion must be constantly prepared to reform itself by harking back to fundamentals, by returning to the original source of knowledge of God.

CHRISTIANITY

The future of Christianity is guaranteed to the satisfaction of all Christians by the truth of the words in the letter to the Hebrews: "Jesus Christ is the same yesterday, today and for ever". That this is not merely a subjective opinion of Christians is evinced by the remarkable fact that Jesus commands respect beyond the bounds of Christianity too. Fierce adversaries of the Church and Christianity have repeatedly expressed their admiration for Jesus and stated their belief that he would have been on their side in the struggle against a corrupt Christianity. It is all the more obvious that Jesus Christ will always remain the spiritual leader of those who name themselves after him. Until the end of time Christianity will be characterized by Christonomy: the word of Christ is the supreme commandment for Christians; his teachings remain the staff of life; as the light of the world he will lead his followers out of the darkness to eternal life.

Yet Christology will likewise remain subject to constant reappraisal and study. This means that theologians must once more render a fresh account of the truths of the gospel. Christian theology has been occupied with the questions this involves for the past nineteen centuries, and during this time it has given admirable proof of its boldness and profundity. Unless the signs are misleading, theology has recently entered a new phase which will demand of its practitioners a high degree of courage and imagination. Christian theology will have to choose an attire in which it can appear before a critical audience without appearing old-fashioned or ridiculous. Such an attire must be capable of making an impression on the present sceptical generation. For the solution of the problems confronting Christianity in its encounter with modern culture and the non-Christian religions the way in which Christianity presents itself is of paramount importance. For this reason a few proposals of a general nature will not be out of place in this final chapter. It should, however, be underlined that a detailed sketch of a new theology is beyond the scope of the present writer and of this book.

A prerequisite for a theology appropriate to the future is a complete revision of all existing notions. One of the principal shortcomings of present-day theology is that, instead of discarding outworn ideas, it refurbishes them time and again. Thus it lags behind the other sciences which are for ever casting aside obsolete theories and thereby rejuvenating themselves. It is without doubt very fascinating to examine old dogmas and creeds and to marvel at the ingenuity of mind and sincerity of belief of those who have gone before us. Indeed, serious students will not fail to gain an understanding of the value of these interpretations of the evangelical truths. Yet we are mistaken and deluded if we imagine that these formulations of Christian belief from bygone times can be imbued with new life as they stand or that we ourselves accept

these beliefs at their face value. It is no more possible
for a Christian of this century to assent to theological
doctrines, built on concepts from a long defunct
world of ideas, than it would be for a man living in a
centrally-heated house fitted out with all the latest
appliances to wish to go back to the primitive dwell-
ings of the Romans, as they are so entertainingly described by Jérôme Carcopino in his *Daily Life in
Ancient Rome*. Attempts to escape from this predica-
ment generally involve such a far-fetched translation
of, say, the dogma of the Trinity, the incarnation, or
the two personalities of Christ that the original
meaning has well nigh vanished. In my opinion these
attempts never do justice to the original significance
of these dogmas, and they also tend to lead to insin-
cerity in religious life.

This does not imply that the fundamental notions
on which these dogmas are built should be aban-
doned. No religion can ever renounce its archetypal pattern without losing its character. As far as
Christianity is concerned this means that it must
remain centred around three ideas: God, the Father,
Christ, the Lord, and the Holy Spirit. Any other
structure of belief is unthinkable. The core of
Christian thinking is and will remain theology,
Christology and pneumatology. What is, however,
questionable is "whether we are prepared for a re-
casting and restatement of Christian truth in the

light of the new knowledge that may come to us."[1]

As for theology in the strict sense of the word, that is as the doctrine concerning God, it should be realized that nothing is to be gained be substituting, as is so often done today, the more clearly focussed image of Christ for the hazy image of God. There are problems relating to God's essence that cannot be solved by Christology. Among these are not only the question, which has been dealt with here, of God's revelation to those living beyond the light shed by the gospel, but also the question of the meaning of creation and of human life with its suffering and wickedness, and last but not least, the question of what place tragedy, chance and many other enigmas of life have in God's purpose for the world. The mysteries of God's essence will never wholly yield to dogmatic formulation. Nevertheless, a bold yet devout attempt will have to be made to carve out an image of God that will serve as a mainstay on which mankind can pin its trust in the paradoxical truth and value of faith, hope and love in a universe filled with demonic obsessions and tragic events.

Christology must choose as its point of departure the role of Saviour that Christ has performed down the centuries. From a purely religious point of view the Saviour is an intermediary: he acts as a bridge be-

[1] Stephen Neill, *Christian Faith and other Faiths, The Christian Dialogue with other Religions*, 1961, p. 292.

tween God and man.[1] This means that he is by definition an exceptional figure, whose essence can never
be grasped within the customary terms which must
have universal validity. His essence is a secret which
we sense, but can never wholly express in words. The
doctrine of the two natures of Christ may be appreciated as a praiseworthy attempt to circumscribe this
secret. This doctrine has become untenable, because
it involves outmoded anthropological conceptions.
To my mind, Christ, the most ancient spiritual title
of honour, is by far the most satisfying theological
designation; for this name originally indicated that
Christ was "anointed" with the spirit of God. He is
the bearer of the Holy Spirit *par excellence*. In Jesus
Christ God's love has been revealed, but not God's un-
fathomable wisdom and majestic omnipotence. His
figure is paradoxical for the simple reason that it was
as the only true King that he served mankind, suffered
and was crucified. The time-worn doctrine of the two
personalities united in Christ no longer adequately
expresses this paradoxicality for anybody with a
measure of understanding of anthropology. It may be
more readily understood that in Jesus Christ two
manners of existence, namely the sacred and the pro-
fane, were harmoniously united in such an exceptional
and miraculous way that he was and still is the "bridge"

[1] C. J. Bleeker, "Die religiöse Bedeutung der Brücke", *The
Sacred Bridge.*

between God and man, because in him we have been granted knowledge of God's mercy and of eternal life. It is this that makes him unique and inspires us to imitate him; that is to practise brotherly love and to take up arms in the struggle against injustice and corruption. Christology has its roots in Christonomy and returns to it time and again.

Christian theology has never succeeded in placing pneumatology in proper perspective. This is not to be wondered at, as the spirit is like the wind: we hear its sound but we know not whence it comes or whither it goeth (John 3.8). We should not, however, allow ourselves to be deterred by the refractoriness inherent in this subject. The Holy Spirit is of cardinal importance, both in Christian religious practice and in Christian thinking. For is it not so that man's rebirth, the regeneration of the world and the vitality of the Church are dependent on the workings of the Holy Spirit? It is therefore necessary for theologians to reflect anew on the function of the Holy Spirit. No one is able to effect the coming of the Holy Spirit. Nevertheless, the significance of this divine power may be explained fairly satisfactorily. In brief, it may be said that there is no hope of sanctification of human life and of the world-order, unless we place our trust in the regenerating powers of the Holy Spirit which emanates from God and of which Jesus Christ is the bearer.

CHRISTIANITY AND THE NON-CHRISTIAN
RELIGIONS

Here we wish to consider the practical application of the ideas advocated in this book. What form should the fraternization between Christians and non-Christians take? To gain a clear idea of this, two facts need to be kept in mind. First, the truth of W. E. Hocking's thesis that Christianity, in its present form at least, is not ready to serve as a religion for the whole world.[1] Christianity no longer has a firm grasp on the masses, it offers no satisfactory solution to the physical needs of our time and it has lost its original moral and spiritual grandeur. These circumstances underline once more the thesis that the gospel is a perilous truth; for the gospel is absolutely binding for all who believe in it. They must stake their lives upon it, whatever the consequences, and despite the fact that they are not entitled either with or without coercion to impose the Christian faith on humanity as the only true faith. Second, our sense of reality should be such that we allow for the actual position of spiritual authority of the non-Christian religions in our own religious outlook and behaviour. There can be no doubt at all that the other world-religions are still spiritual forces which dominate the thoughts and actions of millions

[1] W. E. Hocking, *Living Religions and a World Faith*, 1940, pp. 249f.

of the inhabitants of this earth. For information on
the religious situation in the non-Christian world, the
reader is referred to the relevant literature.[1] One thing,
however, is clear: these religions are by no means
exhausted. They are engaged in a conflict with Western culture, from which they are arising rejuvenated
and even with sufficient vigour to embark on missionary work.[2] A book like *Recovery of faith* by Radhakrishnan is proof that in the East too attempts are
being made to revive true religion.

Considering these facts, it need scarcely be argued
that a world-religion, in which the essential elements
of the various religions are blended together in harmony, is not an ideal to which true Christians and
genuine adherents to other religions can aspire. It
has, indeed, been suggested that the development of
a universal civilization would also bring about the
rise of a universal religion. But as R. L. Slater justly
observes: "the prospect of one world—one religion
is a very remote prospect, to say the least. But the
prospect of one world is not remote."[3] In addition,
Hocking has stressed that religion must, despite its
tendency towards the universal, remain particular,

[1] See for example the books by H. Kraemer mentioned in
Chapter Two; and also P. Tillich, *op. cit.*, pp. 22f.
[2] G. F. Vicedom, *Die Mission der Weltreligionen*, 1959; *Présence
du Bouddhisme*, ed. by René de Berval, 1959.
[3] R. L. Slater, *World Religions and World Community*, 1963, p.
225.

because it expresses the specific convictions of the
believer or the community of believers.[1] So it is, and
so it will remain. Culturally, the inhabitants of our
earth will come more and more to resemble one
another. But neither Christianity nor the other religions can participate in a synthesis without suffering
a loss of character and grandeur. It is precisely in his
beliefs that the man of the future will wish to be himself, because it is solely in the light of what is for him
the ultimate truth that he has come to understand
himself fully. This notion brings us to the realization
that the only correct course of action, with respect to
the problem of the relation between the various religions, is the one recommended by Hocking, namely,
"the way of reconception."[2] As is implied, each religion must rejuvenate and reform itself by harking
back to fundamentals. This reconception, which
should be of an existential rather than an intellectual
nature, is at the same time the best means of fostering
mutual understanding between the adherents of the
diverse religions. The better and more profoundly a
person understands and emotionally experiences his
own religion, the more readily he will understand
others.

In these times of rapid communication, a dialogue
between believers in the East and the West is inevita-

[1] Hocking, *op. cit.*, p. 36.
[2] *Ibid.*, pp. 190f.

ble. The word "dialogue" is so highly rated nowadays
that it would seem to possess magic power. While the
dialogue can indeed smooth the way to better mutual
understanding and appreciation, our expectations as
to the results of such a meeting should not be raised
too high. Despite the prevailing interest in psychology, man's ability to enter into a way of thinking that
is not his own remains restricted. Nevertheless, religious people will be increasingly obliged to discuss
spiritual truths with each other. There is much they
can learn from one another without their having to
renounce any of their distinctiveness. The time has
come for Christianity to acknowledge openly that it
can benefit from certain insights and attitudes inherent
in other religions. Hocking lists the salient conceptions of the non-Christian religions as follows:
"within Islam one is aware of a dignity, a sweep, a
sense of the instant majesty of God, which we lack.
Islam has also an effective fraternity which crosses
racial bounds with an ease which Christianity pro-
fesses but Christians seldom attain." The most admirable features of Hinduism are in his eyes: "the
naturalness of the meditative element of religion",
"the willingness to pay the price of spiritual gifts"
and "the actually achieved serenity of spirit in many
an oriental saint". The characteristic feature of Buddhism is "the enjoyment of the impersonal element of
ultimate truth." The Buddhist realizes that "imperson-

THE FUTURE OF RELIGION

ality belongs to the vast inner spaces of God's being."
The "excellence" of Confucianism is to be found in
"its intense humanity". For the Confucian "the human
bond (is) veritably a way to God", while "the pre-
valent cheerfulness and naturalness of the Confucian
conception of religion" cannot fail to impress outsiders. (op. cit., pp. 254f)

The Christian whose faith is strong can be mag-
nanimous in his recognition of that which is true and
noble in non-Christian knowledge of God. This by
no means relieves him of the duty of testifying to the
truth, which is dear to him above all else. If he is wise he
will testify with deeds rather than words. Anyone at
all familiar with the East knows that opportunities
still exist for Christianity to do valuable work there,
provided that Christians proceed tactfully. Preached
resolutely and with diplomacy, the gospel of Jesus
Christ will bear out the parable of the leavening. Yet
the troubles of the world are numerous. They cannot
all be alleviated by the adherents to one religion. All
believers must form a united front. Their mutual
enemies are poverty, disease, ignorance, injustice and
nihilism.

In his brochure entitled *De drie treden van het volken-
recht* C. van Vollenhoven, the celebrated Dutch authority on international law, has traced the evolution of international law in three distinct phases. The same
process may, to my mind, be observed in the growth

of relations and co-operation between the world-religions. From the Protestant point of view, the development of the oecumenical movement may be seen as the first stage. United in their faith the non-Roman-Catholic churches have learned to co-operate one with another in a spirit of brotherly love. The second phase—the one in which we now find ourselves—is the advance towards agreement between Protestant and Roman-Catholic churches concerning recognition of one another. The mutual distrust and sense of alienation existing between Catholics and Protestants has not yet been dispelled, but closer relations and co-operation between Rome and the Reformation are now only a matter of time. Subsequently, a third and final stage will be entered upon, and in this stage, towards which tentative moves are already being made, the adherents of the various religions will learn to appreciate each other's standpoint and to co-operate on issues of a social and ethical nature. Such a state of affairs may strike the reader as Utopian. But those who believe can afford to wait. They are confident that this will one day be a reality. The logic of the truth which God has revealed to mankind is sweeping us irresistibly towards a condition in which all true believers will be able to understand and appreciate each other's values, without having to relinquish the particular faith that is so dear to them.